Anne F

When Nazi troops invaded Holland and started harassing, torturing, and murdering any Jews they could find, Anne's family and some friends—eight people —hid in the secret annex of a house in Amsterdam. When I visited that house myself a while ago, I couldn't believe that all those people had lived for more than two years in that cramped space. Or that they had lived with such constant fear.

Soldiers were everywhere, you see. As were paid informers. Even before she had moved to the secret annex, Anne had seen more than her share of brutality in her thirteen years—people carted off to die in gas chambers and slave camps, beaten by thugs, robbed of their dignity. And no one knew when or even if World War Two might end.

Yet Anne found a way to hope, sing, and pray all in one: in her diary. Toward the end of her long confinement, she wrote, "It's really a wonder that I haven't dropped all my ideals. . . .Yet, in spite of everything, I still believe that people are really good at heart."

Good at heart. Think of what courage—and hope—it took to say that in the midst of her persecution!

OTHER BOOKS BY T. A. BARRON

The Great Tree of Avalon Trilogy
Child of the Dark Prophecy
Shadows on the Stars
The Eternal Flame

The Heroic Adventures of Kate
Heartlight
The Ancient One
The Merlin Effect

The Lost Years of Merlin Epic
The Lost Years of Merlin
The Seven Songs of Merlin
The Fires of Merlin
The Mirror of Merlin
The Wings of Merlin

Tree Girl

Picture Books
Where Is Grandpa?
High as a Hawk

Visit T. A. BARRON's Web site:
www.tabarron.com

THE
HERO'S
TRAIL

A GUIDE FOR
A HEROIC LIFE

T. A. BARRON

with a preface by Robert Coles, M.D.

PUFFIN BOOKS

PUFFIN BOOKS
Published by the Penguin Group
Penguin Young Readers Group,
345 Hudson Street, New York, New York 10014, U.S.A.
Penguin Group (Canada), 90 Eglinton Avenue East, Suite 700, Toronto, Ontario, Canada M4P 2Y3
(a division of Pearson Penguin Canada Inc.)
Penguin Books Ltd, 80 Strand, London WC2R 0RL, England
Penguin Ireland, 25 St Stephen's Green, Dublin 2, Ireland (a division of Penguin Books Ltd)
Penguin Group (Australia), 250 Camberwell Road, Camberwell, Victoria 3124, Australia
(a division of Pearson Australia Group Pty Ltd)
Penguin Books India Pvt Ltd, 11 Community Centre, Panchsheel Park, New Delhi - 110 017, India
Penguin Group (NZ), Cnr Airborne and Rosedale Roads, Albany, Auckland 1310, New Zealand
(a division of Pearson New Zealand Ltd)
Penguin Books (South Africa) (Pty) Ltd, 24 Sturdee Avenue,
Rosebank, Johannesburg 2196, South Africa

Registered Offices: Penguin Books Ltd, 80 Strand, London WC2R 0RL, England

First published in the United States of America by Philomel Books,
a division of Penguin Putnam Books for Young Readers, 2002
Published by Puffin Books, a division of Penguin Young Readers Group, 2007
10 9 8 7 6

Patricia Lee Gauch, Editor

THE LIBRARY OF CONGRESS HAS CATALOGED THE PHILOMEL EDITION AS FOLLOWS:
Barron, T. A.
The hero's trail : a guide for a heroic life / T. A. Barron ;
with a preface by Robert Coles.
p. cm.
Summary: Explores how to lead a heroic life, facing challenges with courage,
strength of character, and wisdom much as a hiker uses those qualities on a
challenging trail. Includes bibliographical references and index.
ISBN: 0-399-23860-3 (hc)
1. Heroes—Juvenile literature. [1. Heroes. 2. Character. 3. Values. 4. Conduct of life.]
I. Title.
BJ1533.H47 .B29 2002 170'.44—dc21 2002001667

Puffin Books ISBN 978-0-14-240760-8

Printed in the United States of America

The reader's guide was printed with the permission of Dr. Kylene Beers,
Senior Reading Researcher, School Development Program, Yale University.

Contents

for my mother, Gloria Barron,
who taught all her kids the importance of heroes

Preface

What follows are stories about individuals who have made a great moral difference in the lives of so many of us who are eager to find our way through life personally, productively, and not least, meaningfully. T. A. Barron—an American teacher, a one-time businessman, a writer eager to tell us stories, be we children or far along in years—has chosen to look backward and upward in this book. He introduces us to some brave and selfless people from the past who have followed the summons of their conscience, even when such a response has meant death. And we also meet many more people, nearer to our own time, who have stood exceedingly tall ethically, no matter what dangers they faced.

For this book's author—as well as for us, his grateful readers—the "heroic life" of such remarkable people can become a most instructive and helpful guide. As the title of this book reminds us, right off, we can cover great distance while here alive! We hike (as Tom Barron stirs us to consider) across the seasons given us by luck, chance and circumstance. And so we seek directions—not to mention some sense of the overall point of the particular journey that is ours. In a sense, then, this book offers moral companions for this trip we take: people assembled for us to know their lives, their words and their deeds. The result is a psychological and spiritual gift that will enrich us as we head across our given spell of seasons toward that last moment when life departs.

As I read this book, and encountered the honorable and courageous people it celebrates, I marveled at these vulnerable human beings who did so much good, no matter the odds against them. And I recalled the remarks of one of America's finest novelists, Walker Percy, whose novels such as *The Moviegoer* and *The Last Gentleman* are very much devoted to moral as well as social reflection. Once, referring to his effort to connect storytelling to philosophical introspection, Dr. Percy (trained as a physician before he took to the writing life) described a certain routine he'd come upon, as he got ready to sit at his desk and scribble words: "I like to walk off my ideas! I mean, they live in my mind, but it helps me to go use my feet—a way of going from one spot to another. That way, I'm telling myself that the point of the writing is to carry the reader along, move the reader from where he is, she is, to some other place. You stir your imagination and someone else's, and you've got new possibilities about what you might do, could do, and why, and the reasons this voyage (or pilgrimage) makes sense to you."

Such imagery obviously converges with that used in this book—our search for reasons, and for a destination that will, finally, grant us, and those with whom we travel, the moral affirmation that rescues us from the nowhere world of moral oblivion. For Walker Percy, and for this book's author, a life given to careful ethical consideration becomes a journey of time well spent, indeed. On his walks, Tom Barron thought of certain "heroes"—people who gave others a vision of what is desirable, but even more helpful and inspiring, of what is possible. Their decisions made, words spoken, and acts taken, send a loud and clear signal to the rest of us. So as we hike along, take our various steps, choose our own pathways, and keep our eyes open for detours—whether challenging or dangerous, enlivening or deadly—these heroic people will be very much with us. They will be there in our thoughts while we take our promising or perilous strides through life.

The "hero's trail" of this book is meant to be the reader's possible privilege. We are given moral stories, examples, and qualities that will help us be more knowing and kindly every day—both with ourselves, and with others who are near us now and later at our side! Here then, ahead, is a map that graces us with the ideas and ideals of other travelers who dared to put their thinking into action.

Many of us will be glad, for sure, that Tom Barron took the time, and called upon the energy, to connect us to the moral giants in this book. Here is so much grace to regard closely, to hold tight in mind, heart, and soul, as we keep moving on our own hiking trails through life.

—Robert Coles, M.D.

Robert Coles, M.D., child psychologist, is the Pulitzer prize–winning author of *Children of Crisis* and *The Spiritual Life of Children*.

Every great journey begins with a single step.

—Lao-tzu

1 Introduction: The Hero's Hiking Boots

All right, I confess: I absolutely love a good hike. So much that my beat-up old hiking boots practically jump onto my feet and lace themselves whenever I even think about hitting the trail.

For as long as I can remember, it's been that way. Growing up in Colorado ranch country within sight of Pike's Peak didn't hurt. How could anyone resist exploring those rugged ridges, fragrant groves, and high mountain meadows? Trails or no trails, I just had to climb up there.

And so I did. Still do today, in fact—sometimes with one of my own kids strapped to my back. But the more hikes I've taken over the years, the more it seems to me that life *itself* is a remarkable hike. And often . . . a heroic one.

Now wait a minute, you say. Life is some sort of hike? How exactly is that so? And even if it were so, what does it have to do with being a hero? You may be starting to wonder if I've been breathing too much of that thin mountain air.

Think about it, though. Just like life, a hike is a journey—full of ups and downs, long climbs, deep doubts, painful losses, real triumphs, and plenty of surprises. We may make some good friends on the way, but much of the time we walk alone. And as with our own lives, we can't see very far down the trail. We can only keep walking, and do our best to prepare ourselves for whatever twists and turns lie ahead.

Now, to survive that sort of journey, maybe even with grace, we need some essential qualities. Courage, for one. Perseverance. And wisdom. The very same qualities it takes to be a hero.

And so the hero's journey isn't so different from the personal journey that each of us makes through life. Or from a long trip into the wilderness. That's why I think of this book as a hiking guide. Beyond everything else, it's about how you can make your own life a walk on the hero's trail.

What exactly is a hero? What does the word really mean?

Let's start with what a hero does *not* mean: a celebrity. In our society, we often confuse the two, but they are really very different. As different as the two kinds of sage—the person who has grown immensely wise over time, and the sweet but short-lived herb that decorates the prairies.

A hero is someone who, faced with a tough challenge, reaches down inside and finds the courage, strength, and wisdom to triumph. That person could be a girl or a boy; a prominent leader or the person next door; a member of any race, culture, or economic group. But in every case, it's someone whose special qualities of character make a real difference.

A celebrity, by contrast, is just someone who has won our attention—whether for fifteen seconds or fifteen years. The celebrity's fame could have come from entertaining us, serving us . . . or even harming us. Now, don't get me wrong. Sometimes heroes can become so well known that they also become celebrities. Abraham Lincoln was, in his day, both at once. So was Winston Churchill fifty years ago. And so is Jane Goodall today. But the two ideas are still quite different. For a hero, what counts is character. For a celebrity, what counts is fame.

Here's another way to think about it: A hero does something truly important, regardless of whether anyone ever notices. But a celebrity is all about being noticed—being a famous face or name or number on a jersey. One of them, you could say, is a real meal cooking on the campfire. The other is a flash in the pan.

Heroism, then, is about *character*. The qualities a person carries down inside. Or, to put this in hiking terms: The most important piece of equipment that any hiker brings on the trail isn't a backpack, a sleeping bag, or even a map. No, it's the hiker himself or herself! That person's head, heart, and soul. In just the same way, heroes prevail not because of the tools or weapons they carry outside—but because of what they carry *inside*.

Lao-tzu, the Chinese philosopher, pointed out long ago that even the greatest journey begins with a single step. That is true, and well worth remembering. But frankly, I would have said it differently: Every journey begins with a single *person*. A hiker—and whatever inner qualities he or she brings to the trail.

That's true whether the journey is long or short. It could be a full-blown expedition to traverse a whole continent, or a brief side trip to explore a slot canyon. Among the many young heroes we will meet in the coming pages, some embark on lifelong expeditions—to triumph over blindness or polio, to fight discrimination, or to bring a bold new idea into the world. Others take strenuous side trips, ones that require great courage and determination to save someone else's life. But in every case, it's the inner qualities that define the hero—and the hero's journey.

Just how are those inner qualities revealed? Through our choices. For every choice matters, whether it's big or small, conscious or unconscious, repeated or rare. And every choice is an expression of who we are.

Our choices, then, are like footsteps. Each one takes us farther down the trail, affecting the route we take, the pace we set, and the deeds we do along the way. And each one is shaped by two primary forces: our own inner selves, and the trail itself—the landscape of life. So our inner qualities shape our choices; our choices become our footsteps; and our footsteps become our journey.

Sometimes the trail holds surprises. Unexpected turns. We are *forced* to make choices . . . and they're not always easy.

I can't forget the first time, as a teenager, I set out on a long hiking trip alone. My goal was to explore the backcountry for five full days, so I loaded my pack with plenty of food and gear. And I headed deep into the Sangre de Cristo Mountains of southwestern Colorado.

Well, the first day was just drop-your-jaw gorgeous. I hiked through wildflower meadows, over snow-streaked ridges, and down colorful canyons. What a great start to the trip! As the sun went down, I felt good and tired . . . and also hungry. My thoughts turned to cooking up a feast. Big enough for a hungry bear.

That's when I spied a perfect campsite on the other side of a river. Stepping on the mossy stones, I started to cross. Already I could taste that strawberry cobbler I'd be chowing down for dessert. Or maybe for an appetizer! I'd just picked the strawberries, so they couldn't be any fresher.

Suddenly, my foot slipped, and I fell right into the river. My pack came apart and every scrap of gear dumped out. Sleeping bag, clothes, map, everything—completely soaked. And even worse, all my food supplies disappeared, swept away by the rapids.

Good-bye, strawberry cobbler.

Well, that night I tried to fish for supper, using some dental floss for line, an old wire for a hook, and a half-chewed piece of chewing gum for bait. As you might guess, I caught nothing. And ate nothing at all that night.

As I lay in my damp clothes, shivering until dawn, I had to decide whether to head straight back home. Very tempting, believe me! But when I saw the sunrise, glowing all copper and gold, I just couldn't bring myself to leave. So I stayed on that mountainside for two more days—surviving on berries, lichens, and one little grouse egg. It turned out to be a memorable trip after all . . . though the menu was a bit different from what I'd planned.

And so our most intricate plans can be washed downriver when surprises happen. And they do happen! It's how we *respond* to them that's key. (Not to mention how we bait a hook with chewing gum.)

Because any hike has lots of surprises, uncertainties, and

challenges, it helps to think of other people who have walked the same trail before. Trail guides, let's call them. And just as trail guides can be helpful to a hiker on the ground, they can make a crucial difference to anyone on a hero's journey. For they remind us we are not walking alone.

That's one reason heroes are so important. Essential, really. Whether they are real or imaginary, they can guide and encourage us as we follow a heroic trail—climbing a high peak, saving a companion, or enduring a terrible storm.

Maybe that's why I love to read good biographies. Stories about heroic people lift my sights as well as my spirits. And it makes no difference whether those people are still around today or lived thousands of years ago. I'm always inspired by David in the Old Testament when he marches into battle with Goliath, armed only with his slingshot and his faith. Just as I'm always moved by Abraham Lincoln's efforts to hold together the Union with courage and compassion. Then there's Johnny Appleseed, who planted thousands of trees for future generations to enjoy. And Anne Frank, who wrote words so powerful that they have long outlasted Hitler's death camps.

Through biographies, we can always find wisdom in Chief Joseph of the Nez Percé tribe, bravery in Harriet Tubman, ingenuity in Thomas Edison, and leadership in Winston Churchill. And still more inspiration in people such as Mother Teresa, the Dalai Lama, Mohandas Gandhi, Ben Franklin, Jane Goodall, Chico Mendes, Albert Einstein, Eleanor Roosevelt, and Martin Luther King, Jr. These historical figures are trail guides for us all.

We cherish plenty of nonhuman heroes, as well. Take Balto,

the famous sled dog who braved blizzards, frostbite, hunger, and rough terrain to deliver diphtheria medicine just in time to the stricken village of Nome, Alaska. Though his journey happened almost a century ago, we still celebrate it—and take inspiration from it—today.

And let's not forget our many mythic heroes. They range from Prometheus, who sacrificed himself to bring fire to the ancient Greeks, to Coyote, whose wit and nimbleness made him a fixture of Native American tales. There's Anansi, who outwitted the African sky god; Frodo, who emerged from the land of the Hobbits to defeat the powerful Lord of the Rings; Zorro, whose gallantry gave hope to oppressed Mexicans; Princess Leia, whose bravery in *Star Wars* helped save an entire galaxy; and King Arthur, who created the realm of Camelot, a place that has lived in people's hearts for more than a millennium. And so many, many more!

All these legendary heroes can guide us on the trail. And here's the best part: It really doesn't matter whether their stories are based on fact, hearsay, or fiction. What matters is that all these people represent some heroic quality that we admire. That we seek in ourselves. It could be courage, honesty, persistence, humor, compassion, or something else. By celebrating the hero, we are also celebrating the quality that he or she stands for.

And so today, when you and I sit by a campfire and tell tales of heroic people, we are part of a long tradition. One that connects our campfire to all those ancient flames that have burned in Celtic fire circles, Tibetan hearths, Native American kivas, or prehistoric cave dwellings. And that connects our tales to those from every place and time—what Joseph Campbell called "the one, shape-shifting yet marvelously constant story."[1]

Let's imagine the scene: You, a young man or woman, are sitting on a stone by the campfire. Kneeling by the flames am I—an old friend of the family. And you are both excited and scared about tomorrow's hike up the mountain. Just as I was, years ago, when I made that same hike. You know it won't be easy, but you don't really want to talk about your fears. And so in silence, we cook some thick stew and bake a pair of apples with honey and cinnamon. Then, as the sky darkens, something remarkable happens.

Our campfire burns low. It snaps and sputters as the coals warm our hands.

"Toss a fat one on there, would you?" I wave at the woodpile.

You nod, but stay quiet, still thinking about tomorrow's climb. Though your face is in shadow, I can see the anxiousness in your eyes. Just as you reach for some firewood, a shaggy dog bounds over. He grabs a hefty branch in his teeth and carries it to me.

"Thanks, Herc." I rub his neck.

Hercules shakes his head, flapping his ears against his snout. He nuzzles my leg, and then yours. But you don't seem to notice.

I toss the branch onto the flames. Sparks rise, glowing like newborn stars. Higher they float, and higher, into the night sky. And so the stars of Earth and Heaven mingle for a moment. Then, one by one, the sparks wink out. Seconds later, they are gone. Their ashes drift slowly down to the fire and disappear.

You shift on your stone, then speak at last. "How about a story?"

"Sure. With a hero?"

"Yes, a hero." You glance in the direction of the ridge above us, and almost smile. "One who climbs a great big mountain."

Now, no scene is more human than that. A challenge looms, and so do your doubts. Then a story is told, a hero celebrated. And you know you're not the first person to walk on that trail.

And here's something wonderful: Heroes are more than companions on our journey. They remind us who we are, and who we can become. In truth, when we follow the hero's trail, we are entering into ourselves—into our hopes, struggles, fears, and ideals. Celebrating heroes is a terrific way to remember *our own* heroic potential.

That's why we need our heroes. Yes, today more than ever. We need to know them, think about them, and honor them. For they remind us how far we can go. How high we can climb.

All that's fine, you might be thinking. But we still need to answer two fundamental questions: What does it really take to be a hero? And who gets to be one?

Those are things I've wondered about, too, over many years. Perhaps that's why, as a writer, I am so drawn to heroic characters. In fact, when I'm not writing nature books about Colorado (which, if nothing else, give me a good reason to take a hike), I am writing about heroes.

Take, for example, Kate—the gritty, adventurous girl I describe in *Heartlight* and other novels. Now, she would be the last person to call herself a hero. Or special in any way. Yet every time she winds up in trouble—which, believe me, is often—she finds out that she has the inner qualities that she needs to triumph.

The same is true for the young boy who washes ashore on the first page of *The Lost Years of Merlin*, and who finally becomes the mentor of King Arthur and the greatest wizard of all times. But when the sea hurls his body ashore, young Merlin is so weak he can hardly breathe. He has no memory at all, and no reason to hope that he'll survive that terrible day. And yet . . . he has something else down inside. Something truly heroic. That's what carries him through that day—and into his wondrous destiny.

In the years since these books were published, I have been asked again and again, by people of all ages, what it really takes to be a hero. What does the word actually mean? What is its essence, its core? Even . . . its secret? By the end of this book, I hope the answers will be clear.

Many people wonder about something else, as well—whether they, too, have what it takes to be a hero. Whether they, too, can do something heroic in their own lives. Or is that whole idea just nonsense? A notion that works in stories about imaginary people, but not in real life?

Well, my answer to that question is simple: *Everyone* can be a hero.

Girl or boy, rich or poor, old or young—it doesn't matter. Heroes can be any gender. Or any race. They can come from any cultural background or economic circumstance. And so, in the following chapters, you will meet many young heroes, as varied as can be, who look like every strain of humanity.

And you'll also meet some heroes whose names you haven't heard before. That's because even though we often sing the praises of heroes, some of our *greatest* heroes are completely unsung. Even unknown. Think of the single mom who devotes her life to helping her kids. The firefighter who dashes into a burning building. Or the student who stands up to a brutal bully. Such people may not seem like anything unusual . . . but they are heroes indeed. That is, if we define heroes by their qualities of character—not by their outward appearance or fame.

On September 11, 2001, when this book was nearly finished, Americans suffered an attack by terrorists driven by arrogance, hatred, and cowardice. Those attackers destroyed thousands of people's lives, as well as the World Trade Center in New York, and part of the Pentagon in Washington, D.C. But they didn't come close to destroying the heroism of the American people. And so, despite the anguish caused by that one act of terror, Americans responded with literally *millions* of acts of courage, generosity, loyalty, hope, and perseverance. Many of those acts are known to just a handful of people; some will never be known at all. Yet they are no less heroic.

This basic idea that heroism is about character, more than anything else, explains how I've chosen the heroes who will be our trail guides for this book. Many people divide heroes into groups based on whether they are famous or unknown; real or imaginary; historical or contemporary. But such divisions miss the point. For anyone with the right qualities can be a hero.

And so, in the pages to come, I will do exactly the opposite.

It is my intention to mix together all sorts of heroic people. You will find ordinary folks alongside figures from legend and myth, ancient heroes alongside modern ones. That's because I want to emphasize that anyone can be a hero. Today's unsung heroes could be tomorrow's legends. And who knows? Maybe you yourself will be among them.

Now, I *will* divide heroes into five different types. But my categories aren't based on what people looked like, when they lived, or how their stories began. No, my categories are based on what kinds of *character* they displayed.

In the next five chapters, you will meet the hero on the spot, the survivor hero, the hero within, the hero to others near and far, and the hero for all time. They are five distinct ways to be a hero. Or, you could say, five distinct ways to walk on the hero's trail. In each case, the trail leads to higher ground. But in each case, the hero faces a different kind of challenge—and needs a different combination of qualities to triumph.

Sometimes, of course, these qualities overlap. Different types of heroes may show similar virtues. Courage, for example. All of them show incredible guts—whether it's the courage to save someone from drowning, to speak out against bulldozers that are about to destroy a forest, or to survive an avalanche. And none of these forms of courage is superior to the rest.

So why make these categories at all? Because by focusing on five kinds of challenges—and the heroes they produce—we can explore what qualities of character are essential to heroism. We can see some of the ways heroes are similar, and also different. And we can get to the bottom of that fundamental question: *What does it really take to be a hero?*

And now . . . are you ready to hike? Let's first check our gear. For this trip we won't need the usual stuff—boots, sleeping bag, tent. No, the hero's journey requires different things altogether. Perseverance, for a start. Plus plenty of courage, creativity, and faith. Also a sense of what's right, a touch of wonder, and as much humility as we can carry. And, of course, that essential survival tool: a sense of humor.

All right, then! Let's hit the trail.

I am grateful for the courage of youth.

—Eleanor Roosevelt

2 Hero on the Spot

All through the morning we hike. Shafts of light slice through dark spruces. Resins, tart and sweet, fill the air. The trail seems very quiet . . . though every few minutes a wild mountain wind comes out of nowhere, shaking the treetops and sprinkling us with needles.

No matter how fast you and I walk, Herc always goes faster. He bounds ahead, both ears flapping. When he gets too far ahead, he lopes back. Then he bounds off again. By now, I figure, he's covered at least twice our distance.

"Time to eat!" you announce.

"For a kid like you, it's always time to eat." I nod at the rushing creek just ahead. "Let's cross over and then find a place for lunch. But first I need to get this stone out of my boot."

"All right. I'll go ahead and find a good spot. But don't take forever. I'm starving."

"Quick as a wink," I reply.

"I just winked," you say with a grin. "Done yet?"

"No!" My voice is half growl, half laugh. "Get going, will you? I'll catch up."

You stride off. I lean back against an old spruce tree that creaks with every gust of wind, and start unlacing my boot.

At that instant, a powerful gust rips through the trees. It shrieks like a locomotive. Branches sway and rattle; cones litter the ground. My own tree bends— then suddenly snaps. Shards of wood shoot into the air.

I dive out of the way, but not fast enough. A huge branch crashes down on my chest! I struggle to lift it. But no—too heavy. It's hard to breathe. Even a little. "Help!" I cry, hoping you'll hear. But my voice is swallowed by the wind.

Again, I try to shove the branch aside. No use. I twist, trying to wriggle out from under its weight. Pain burns through my chest. I can't move. Can't breathe . . .

Just then you dash toward me. You grab the branch and heave. Slowly, it budges, then lifts. It's off! All I can do is gasp for air.

"Don't worry," you say. "We'll get you out of here." You try your best to smile. "Quick as a wink."

The hero on the spot. One instant you're a companion, or even just a passerby—and the next instant you're called on to help. To save someone's life.

This kind of hero is created in a heartbeat. And usually, as in the hiking episode above, there is no warning. Everything around you seems calm. Quiet. And then—an emergency explodes right in your face.

That moment of crisis is all it takes to change an ordinary, everyday person into a hero on the spot. That is, if he or she has the right qualities. But here's something fascinating about this kind of hero: It's very hard to know if a person has the makings of one before the crisis actually happens.

Take, for example, the final voyage of the *Titanic*. In the frenzied moments before the great ship sank, many passengers panicked. Because there weren't enough lifeboats to go around, some people trampled others to get on board. Others, who had already found a lifeboat, used oars to beat off any newcomers. And yet . . . at the very same time, some passengers volunteered to stand aside so that others could be saved. Some even led more feeble people into lifeboats, then went back to help again.

What made the difference? What made it possible for some people, on that terrible night in the North Atlantic, to act heroically?

Character, certainly. At the most instinctive level. For this kind of hero has no time for deep reflection or thoughtful plans. In a crisis, it's now or never. Under that sort of pressure, how a person acts is determined by the fundamental makeup of his or her character.

But exactly which qualities of character are we talking about? And how did they get there? Let's look at two examples of heroes on the spot—one from history and one from legend—to find some clues.

One day in 1613, crisis suddenly struck the village of a Native American girl named Pocahontas. Her name meant *playful one* in the language of her people, the Potomac tribe of Chesapeake Bay. But on that day, when she was just twelve years old, Pocahontas was forced to choose between her playful ways and something deadly serious.

It probably started out like an ordinary morning. Pocahontas would have been doing her morning chores, gathering corn or weaving a basket, when suddenly shouts filled the air. Tribal warriors had captured John Smith, leader of the settlers who had established the new outpost of Jamestown, Virginia. Though the tribe had been friendly at first to the newcomers, goodwill had given way to mistrust. Now Smith, judged guilty of trying to destroy the tribe, was being dragged to his death. Seconds later, Chief Powhatan—the father of Pocahontas—raised his stone club to smash the intruder's head.

Pocahontas could have just ignored the whole thing. After all, she had plenty of chores to do. And besides, Smith was an invader. Not to mention a white man, who wore strange garb and spoke a whole different tongue. And who was Pocahontas to interfere with the tribal elders? With her own father?

So many reasons to do nothing! Yet Pocahontas had a choice. To act or not. To walk the tougher trail—or stay safely uninvolved. And she had just an instant to decide.

My guess is that she realized that this man, for all his strangeness, was still a man. A human being, like herself. And if she didn't help him—right then on the spot—no one else would. So she dashed over and threw herself in front of him.

After a tense moment, her father lowered his club. John Smith lived.

Now, let's compare the heroism of Pocahontas with that of a fabled boy known as Peter of Holland. According to the old Dutch tale, Peter also faced a split-second decision: whether to try to stop a dike from bursting that could flood his whole village. Like Pocahontas, he could have turned his back on the crisis. But something down inside wouldn't let him.

It was early evening, almost suppertime, when Peter spied the hole in the dike that held back the sea. Young as he was, Peter knew that if the hole spread, the wall would burst and seawater would come crashing through. Many lives and homes could be lost.

On the other hand, he was just a boy. And fixing a dike was definitely adult work. He'd seen teams of grown men and women struggling to haul stones and pour vats of mortar. Besides, the sun had set and it was getting cold. His parents would soon be missing him. And the streets were empty. No one would ever know if he just kept walking.

But Peter thrust his finger into the dike. And he stayed there, teeth chattering, through the long night. He must have felt sure morning would never come. Yet it finally did, along with others who could help. And so Peter saved his village.

Now, both of these stories have been told and retold many times, made into books and plays and films. They are almost clichés. But why? What is it about these two tales that keeps them alive?

Well, for starters, they are just plain gripping stories. Both involve a brave young hero who takes action—whether he or she is helping a single person or a whole village, a total stranger or a hometown. And both involve the drama of a split-second choice, making them suspenseful and exciting tales.

But something deeper is going on. There are plenty of suspenseful stories that don't lodge so deeply in people's hearts. The tales of Pocahontas and Peter, and others like them, have taken on lives of their own because they say some crucial things about heroes—especially heroes on the spot.

First, they point out the essential power of choice. Both Pocahontas and Peter faced clear options. Stark consequences. And almost no time to decide. The pressure to act in a split second highlights the importance, as well as the difficulty, of making choices. At the same time, it reminds us that we always have that power. Always.

Second, they affirm some values we cherish. In the case of these young heroes—as with all heroes on the spot—their actions show the twin virtues of courage and compassion. Together, those virtues produce someone who is willing to risk serious harm to help someone else.

Amazingly, all this happens in a heartbeat. More than anything else, it's the sheer *intensity* of this kind of heroism that sets it apart. While heroic situations often involve crucial choices, as well as courage and compassion, for the hero on the spot these elements are telescoped down to a single instant. At most, a few minutes.

That's one reason this kind of hero is so striking—and so compelling. What happens to the hero in that intense, concentrated moment reveals a lot about who that person really is. In the same way a big pot of broth can be boiled down to a small cube of bouillon, a sudden emergency tends to boil you or me down to our essential selves.

Hold on, though. Just how did those essential qualities get there in the first place? And how did they become so deeply ingrained in the hero on the spot that they made all the difference in a crisis? To begin to answer these questions, let's meet some contemporary heroes.

When Sherwin Long of Boston, Massachusetts, was nine years old, he couldn't swim. Sometimes he would splash around in the shallow end of a swimming pool with his six-year-old brother, Joshua. But deep water? Forget it.

All that changed suddenly one day when Sherwin, playing near a pool, heard some shouts. He whirled around. Then his heart sank. "It was my brother, Joshua, struggling in the deep end of the pool." *The deep end.*

Sherwin didn't take time to think about his fears. Not him! He plunged right in, trying to reach Joshua. "I yelled for my mother as I headed for him. I tried to run in the water, which was

SHERWIN LONG

almost impossible. . . . I finally got to him, pushed him with all my might, and my mother grabbed him."

Can you imagine how Sherwin felt, seeing his brother pulled to safety? He'd done it! Then, all of a sudden, he realized he had another problem: He was in the deep end himself. Somehow, he struggled over to the side. He wrote, "I crawled out of the pool feeling like my heart was about to burst, I was so scared."[2]

This young hero found a way to save his brother. And he also found something else—a sense of his own heroic qualities.

Like Sherwin, Melinda Clark didn't have time to ponder her fears. But she did have time to act. And to save some lives in the process.

Melinda, age thirteen, woke up on a cold winter night in Everett, Pennsylvania. Except she wasn't cold. Her room felt unusually warm . . . and smoky. The house was on fire!

Melinda's two-year-old brother, Justin, ran into her room, shouting. Out in the hallway, flames leaped and smoke billowed. She dashed to her bedroom window, followed by Justin, along with their sister Courtney, age four, and brother Wayne, age twelve. But the window, warped from the growing heat, wouldn't budge. Melinda pushed harder—and it finally opened. The children hustled out onto the roof ledge.

Suddenly Melinda realized that Justin wasn't with them. He was still inside the burning house!

Though smoke poured out the window and sparks flew into the night sky, Melinda crawled back inside. All the smoke made her drop to her knees on the hot carpet. At last she found her little brother, huddled under her bed. Her eyes and throat burned, but she carried him back outside. Suddenly her foot broke through the roof. It was melting! Quickly, she dropped the little ones into the snow below, before leaping down herself. Just then her mother ran over to hug her children—all safe, thanks to Melinda.

Now, Melinda suffered some burns. And some dreadful

memories of the fire. But here is what her brother Justin remembered about that night: "An angel picked me up and threw me out the window. It was a real angel. I know it."[3]

And who could disagree?

Somehow, when crises struck, Sherwin and Melinda were *ready*. In the same way that an apple seed, no bigger than a freckle, is ready to sprout into a great tree. All it takes is the right environment—soil, water, and sunlight—and the transformation occurs. For inside that tiny brown case is everything needed to produce a trunk taller than three grown people. As well as thousands of sweet

MELINDA CLARK

blossoms, loads of fruit, and countless new seeds, year after year after year.

"Readiness is all," said Shakespeare. But what factors make someone ready to sprout into a hero on the spot?

Being prepared can help. I remember looking forward to family camp-outs as a kid. After all . . . here was my big chance to get bruised, scraped, frostbitten, worn out, eaten by bugs, and covered with mud—all in one weekend! Maybe that was why my dad took such great pains to be prepared. He'd stuff his backpack with an emergency room's worth of bandages, ointment, tape, splints, and other first-aid gear. Just in case.

Still, being ready on the conscious level is not enough. And it's no use at all if a person isn't also ready at the deeper, subconscious level. For emergencies test our most unyielding strengths, our most fundamental values. They tell us, in a flash, whether we are an apple seed, an acorn . . . or a stone.

The ultimate readiness lies in the realm of the soul. A person's genes, personality, and divine spirit all play a part. And so do the many influences of a lifetime: Was the potential hero ever helped by someone else? Loved deeply by someone else? Did he or she ever show signs of courage at earlier times? We are shaped by every one of our experiences, discoveries, mentors, stories, successes, failures, hopes, beliefs, and aspirations.

Taken all together, these elements can produce a soul that is ready at the most fundamental level. A soul strengthened by courage. And deepened by compassion. Do we have, at last, everything we need for a hero on the spot?

Not quite.

There is one final quality that this kind of hero requires. Without it, Melinda Clark probably couldn't have saved her brother, and Peter of Holland couldn't have lasted through the long, cold night.

Perseverance. What my dad used to call "stick-to-it-ivity." It's the ability to stay on the trail you've chosen, no matter how rocky or steep or difficult it becomes. Because of the sheer intensity of emergency situations, this sort of perseverance may take only a small amount of time—but an enormous amount of determination. Heroes on the spot may be no braver than the average person. But they *are* often brave for a few minutes longer.

And that few minutes can make all the difference.

Take the case of Tiare Marie Wells, a student at Colorado State University in Fort Collins. While on vacation during the winter, Tiare passed by a frozen reservoir, and three men fishing through the ice. Curious about the sport—so different from fly-fishing—she climbed out of her car and chatted with one of them, a man named Monte Bassett. After a few minutes, she said good-bye to Monte and turned to go.

Suddenly she heard shouts. The ice had cracked! Two of the men plunged into thirty-eight-degree water, dragged down by their heavy clothes. Monte struggled to pull them out when the ice broke under him, too. He tumbled into the widening hole. Now all three men flailed and shouted, fighting for their lives.

Tiare hovered at the edge, not knowing what to do. If she went too close to them, she could easily fall through the ice herself. But she had to do something. Her mind raced. Then she remembered: She had a horse halter in the back of her car. Just maybe . . .

She ran to the car, snatched the halter, dashed back, and threw it out to the men. Monte grabbed hold, as the others clung to him. And then Tiare pulled. And pulled. "It didn't go through my head that I'd fall in, too," she explained afterward. "I just reacted to them needing help. . . . They kept going under." Her whole body ached from the strain, but she refused to quit: "I don't know where I got the strength. . . . Monte was holding on for dear life."[4]

Finally, she pulled Monte out of the near-freezing

Photograph courtesy of Stephen Collector

TIARE MARIE WELLS

water. Though his two companions drowned, he survived. And lived to see another day. All because of a brave young woman who just wouldn't let go.

Daniel Lopez-Galvan showed the same sort of perseverance one day in 1995. As a teenager, he hadn't been a licensed driver for long when his mother asked him to drive their family home from a Thanksgiving weekend. That afternoon on the highway, traffic was heavy but moving slowly. All of a sudden, the RV in front of them swerved out of control and crashed into an oncoming car. The RV exploded into flames, while the other car rolled several times and finally stopped, flipped over on its roof. Daniel pulled over and ran down the highway to help the people in the overturned car.

"The driver and passenger in the front seat were crushed, but I looked in the backseat and saw a girl's blond hair hanging down."[5] While Daniel struggled to free the girl, gasoline poured out of the car's tank, soaking the ground. With the RV burning nearby, the whole car—and Daniel himself—could go up in flames any moment.

But he didn't quit, even as flames swept nearer. The air smelled of gasoline. His mother shouted at him to get out of there. Still, he kept working to pull the girl from the wreckage. Her arms. Her torso. Finally! Daniel dragged her to safety. This determined young man had succeeded . . . and someone else had lived.

In closing, it's worth mentioning one more thing about heroes on the spot. Before a moment of crisis, they seem like perfectly ordinary folks, going through life in an ordinary way. They wear no special clothes, and have no special training.

They look like you or me or someone we might pass on the street. And they probably don't consider themselves unusually brave or wise or gifted.

Then a crisis explodes. And these heroes step forward to save someone's life. All because they had the crucial qualities inside. And because they happened to be right there—on the spot.

More Heroes on the Spot . . .

Derek Loman, a high school freshman in Washoe Valley, Nevada, saved a seventy-nine-year-old man from being mauled by a crazed dog. Though the man weighed more than Derek, the boy managed to drag him away from the dog and lift him over a five-foot-high fence to safety. Derek's courage and quick action saved someone sixty-five years older than himself.[6]

Ruben Ortega, a student at San Gabriel High School in California, bravely protected his classmates from a boy who had threatened them with a gun. After the incident, Ruben's principal, Jack Mount, said: "I wouldn't have picked Ruben out in a crowd as a hero. But I think heroes are often like that."[7] How true! You can't tell heroes by how they look, but by how they act under pressure.

Sheherazade was a legendary Arabian girl whose on-the-spot heroism saved her sister's life. And others, as well. When she discovered that her beloved sister was about to marry the king—a tyrant who always beheaded his wives on the morning after their wedding—Sheherazade moved fast. She swapped herself for the bride, thus rescuing her sister. Then, following the wedding, she started to tell the king a wondrous tale that lasted the whole night through. He was so captivated by her story that when morning came he couldn't possibly kill her. She kept telling fabulous yarns, one after another, night after night—the stories known today as The Arabian Nights. At last, the king realized his folly and promised to end his cruel ways. Sheherazade had triumphed.

Carl Boney and **Michael Etowski,** both age fourteen, were riding home on the school bus in Fayetteville, North Carolina—when crisis struck. Without warning, the bus driver passed out, and the vehicle careened toward some trees. The two boys rushed forward, steered the bus clear of danger, and finally pulled over. As children screamed and cried around them, Carl helped everyone off. Meanwhile, Mike used his Boy Scout first-aid training to treat the driver for shock. Medics arrived and took the man, who had suffered a stroke, to the hospital. Later, Carl dismissed any praise, saying, "What we did was natural." Mike agreed: "We're just ordinary boys."[8] Maybe so . . . but they're also heroes.

Esther, one of the Bible's bravest heroes, had to act swiftly when she discovered a plot to kill all the Jews in the Persian kingdom ruled by her husband, Ahasuerus. She knew that only the king himself could stop the plot, which had been hatched by his advisor, Haman. But in that realm, anyone who dared to appear before the king without first being summoned would be killed. Even so, Esther knew that if she didn't act right away, many innocent men, women, and children would perish. And since she herself was Jewish, she was willing to take a great risk for her people. So she sought out the king. To her relief, he spared her and even welcomed her, and she told him about Haman's crimes. The king ended the plot and the Jewish people were saved. Or, as the Scripture says, they "had light, and gladness, and joy, and honour."[9] All thanks to Esther's heroism on the spot.

That which we are, we are;
One equal temper of heroic hearts,
Made weak by time and fate, but strong in will—
To strive, to seek, to find, and not to yield.

—Alfred Tennyson, "Ulysses"

③ Survivor Hero

A stairway of flowers—that's what this trail feels like all summer long. But not now. All those September blizzards have covered the ridge in snow. Now, instead of colorful flowers, all we see is white.

My foot breaks through. I'm in snow up to my hips. "Not again!"

You reach to help me. "These drifts are bad, all right. But hey, we can't turn back now. We're so close."

"It's not the drifts that bother me." We both knew the real problem was the avalanche danger.

"Come on, now," you insist, helping me climb back onto the crust. "Remember that line from Tennyson you're always quoting? 'To strive, to seek . . . but not to yield.' "

"Oh, all right. We're almost at the top. But then we—"

A sudden jolt rocks the ridge. We grab each other, barely keep our balance. Right above us, a tall drift falls over in a swirl of snow. Then—a loud boom, like a cannon. And with a deafening roar, the whole ridge slides downward. Tons and tons of snow everywhere! The avalanche slams into us, hurling our bodies down the slope.

Suddenly: stillness. The snow around me lurches, then locks into place. I can't see, can't move. I'm buried! Struggling, I lower my hands that had shielded my face. It looks lighter up above, so maybe I'm near the surface. Got to climb out. Quickly, before I freeze. I twist my shoulders, pushing back the snow. My hands throb with cold. But I start to climb. Snow coats my eyes, my face, but I keep clawing higher.

My tunnel collapses and I tumble backward. Panting, I shiver in a heap. No feeling at all now in my hands. And I'm so tired. How good it would feel to rest, for just a little . . . But no, can't rest. Can't! Got to climb again. Very slowly, I move higher. My arms ache, my legs feel like slabs of ice.

One last time, I swing my hand over my head. Daylight! A rush of air. And then a hand—your hand. Grabbing my own.

Relieved, you hug me, and say just two words: "You survived."

Survivor heroes usually don't start the day expecting to face a life-or-death disaster. Just the opposite. They just take their normal trail, one they've walked many times before. Then, suddenly, the ground shifts beneath their feet. The world comes crashing down like an avalanche. And they must fight for their lives.

Such disasters might come from nature—a hurricane, flood, or lightning bolt. Or from man, as when a drunk driver crashes into a bus loaded with children. Or from nature and man combined, as when forested hills are clear-cut, causing landslides that bury people and homes.

What keeps someone alive who is shipwrecked by a storm, crushed under a car, or buried under a pile of snow? For a start, most survivors have a deep, primal desire to live. To see another day. *To take another breath.*

The will to live. It's a powerful force—as strong, in its way, as any avalanche. Often, it's tied to someone or something specific: a person you want to see again, a place you want to go. Or even, as we'll see in this chapter, a food you want to eat. But most of all, it's about being alive. Seeing, touching, laughing, crying—and breathing.

But even the will to live, by itself, is not enough. People who survive something terrible often need additional, special qualities. That's true for heroes who triumph over challenges from *outside* themselves, such as the young people in this chapter who survive being lost, abandoned, or persecuted. And it's also true for those heroes who triumph over challenges from *inside* themselves—blindness, cystic fibrosis, or polio—whom we'll meet in the next chapter.

In this way, survivor heroes are like every other kind of hero: They must reach down inside to find the special qualities it takes to prevail. What those qualities are, and why they make survival possible, is what this chapter is about.

Here's a brainteaser to start with:

Think of all your favorite people, the ones dearest to your heart. Mom, Dad, sister, brother, friend, whoever. And do you have any beloved pets? Add them in, too. Now think of all the little comforts and rhythms of your life that you enjoy—that morning hug from someone special, that comfy chair by the window, that chocolate-chip cookie right out of the oven.

Now . . . take them all away. Make them vanish! Imagine your life, all alone, with none of those people, places, or things. And imagine how you would survive.

That's what really happened to a boy named Ben MacDonald. You see, back in 1870, when Ben was only six, he wandered off his parents' farm near Winnipeg, Canada. And in those days, leaving the farm meant entering the wilderness.

It was June, and buffalo grass waved in the wind. Ben just couldn't resist climbing over the farmyard fence. He didn't worry that his parents had told him to stay nearby, or that he'd heard the wolves howling at night. He'd be back long before supper. Besides, Ben had a special talent. Whether clucking with the chickens or sidling up to a strange dog, he could communicate with animals—better, maybe, than with people. So he didn't fear whatever creatures lived beyond the fence.

Well, that whole afternoon Ben roamed over the prairie. He followed the tracks of a doe and fawn, caught a turtle down by the stream, and found the nest of a grouse. Then, without warning, a storm erupted. Hailstones pounded his back, sleet bit into his cheeks. He needed someplace to hide! He must have started to run, but tripped on a hole, twisting his ankle badly. So badly he couldn't walk.

The storm blew fiercer. Lightning exploded. Desperately, Ben clawed at the mud around the hole until it was big enough to crawl inside. Though his ankle throbbed, and the space underground was cramped, at least he was safe and dry. What luck! He'd found an abandoned badger's den.

Except that it wasn't abandoned. Later that night, Ben awoke to the sound of an angry beast snarling at him. Only inches away from his face! And Ben had no room to back away or even turn around.

Now, at the MacDonald farm, days went by with no sign of Ben. His parents and his older brother searched frantically for him. Neglecting their farmwork, they spent up to twenty hours a day combing the prairie and the forest lands beyond. With no luck at all. As the days turned into weeks, they finally gave up hope. No six-year-old could survive so long without food or shelter in the wilderness. Probably he'd fallen prey to wolves or a bear. Or simply starved to death.

You can imagine the MacDonalds' shock when, more than two months later, Ben returned to the farm. Alive. For most of the summer, he had lived with the female badger whose den he had found. She had essentially adopted him, taking care of him while his ankle healed. She'd brought him food—prairie mice, lemmings, leopard frogs—when he wasn't able to hunt himself. And then, after he could walk again, he had stayed with the badger for a while, learning her ways and surviving in her world.

Ben's story, amazing as it sounds, is true. (If you'd like to read a gripping account, check out *Incident at Hawk's Hill*, by Allan W. Eckert.) And Ben's experience points out the first key quality of survivors: adaptability. To survive in the badger's environment, Ben learned to eat uncooked frogs, sleep underground, and talk in grunts and chatters. He learned how to hunt by crawling so slowly and quietly that he could surprise even a field mouse. And how to sense an oncoming storm by the slightest prickling of his hair.

This kind of ability to adapt reminds me of Mafatu, the Polynesian boy who is the hero of *Call It Courage*. He's one of my favorite legendary characters—mainly because he adapted so brilliantly. For even though his name meant *stout heart*, to everyone else on the isle of Hikueru, he was a coward. Ever since his mother had drowned at sea, Mafatu feared its crashing waves, sudden storms, and black depths. And he felt shamed by his fear.

Finally, to prove himself, he faced the sea—alone. On a small canoe carved from a tamanu tree, he rigged a cloth sail and set out for the open ocean. Day after day he sailed, surviving violent storms, brutal sun, and worst of all, his nightmares of Moana, the terrible sea god who had killed his mother. At last, a monstrous wave ripped the paddle from his hands and splintered his craft. Mafatu, nearly drowned, washed ashore on a strange island. To stay alive, he figured out how to spear a fish, build a fire, and weave a tent from palm fronds. After months of surviving, he even plunged deep into the water and held his breath long enough to battle *feké*, the deadly octopus.

At long last, he returned to Hikueru. As soon as he landed on the beach, his father embraced him and cried, "Here is my son come home from the sea! Mafatu, Stout Heart. A brave name for a brave boy."[10]

Now here's another amazing example of adaptability: a

young man named Ohiyesa. Born a Santee Sioux in the Minnesota territory in 1858, he spent a traditional childhood with his tribe. He learned how to hunt deer with a bow and arrow, and how to use every scrap of his prey from hooves to hide to bladder. He learned the sacred chants and dances of his people, as well as the calls of ravens, wolves, and black bears.

Then, in his fourteenth year, everything suddenly changed. His father, who had been taught by missionaries, tore Ohiyesa away from the tribe. He made the boy renounce his Sioux heritage, and promise never to speak his old language again. They moved to a frontier settlement, where the boy started all over. New words, new clothes, new school. And even a new name, for now he became Charles Eastman.

Can you imagine how hard that must have been? His whole world just vanished—and was replaced by another, very strange one, with none of his old friends, places, or customs. And yet this capable young man survived. Not only that, he mastered English and his studies so well that he went on to college and eventually medical school.

Finally, he became a doctor. Determined to help his people in any way possible, he went to work at the Sioux reservation in Pine Ridge, South Dakota. Despite the rampant disease and poverty, he managed to save many lives, including some after the Wounded Knee Massacre. And that's not all. He became a nationally

CHARLES EASTMAN

known writer and speaker, publishing ten books and many articles that promoted the honor and dignity of Native Americans.[11]

Now, Charles Eastman showed impressive adaptability. But he also showed some other important qualities of character—qualities crucial to any survivor. To understand what they are, let's look at some more examples. And let's start with a brave young lad named Joshua Dennis.

One day in 1989, when Joshua was ten, he went with his Scout troop to explore an old mine called Hidden Treasure, located near Stockton, Utah. Despite the many dangers of abandoned mines, the group ventured down into the long, damp tunnels. But Joshua, who was younger than the other boys, had trouble keeping up. He tripped over some rocks—and got separated from the group.

Suddenly he was all alone. Worse yet, he was two thousand feet inside a mine, with no light, no water, and no food. He called for help. No one answered. He tried to follow the tunnel, but slammed his head on the jagged ceiling. Then, despite the total blackness of the mine, he found some old railroad tracks and followed them to a steep pile of rubble that led him to a ledge. Tired, damp, and sore, he stopped there to wait for help.

Well, Joshua waited. And waited. And waited. For five whole days he huddled there by himself. Just imagine what it was like: Totally dark. Totally alone . . . except for the rats and bats who rustled past every so often. For five days.

Think he was hungry? You bet! So hungry he started dreaming about food. Once he even dreamed he was eating a French fry smothered in ketchup, then awoke to find it was really just a muddy rock! There he was, trying to chew on a stone. Not a very satisfying meal.

But Joshua didn't give up. He prayed that someone would find him. And he did something else, something that showed his true inner strength. He sang! Right there in the pitch black of the mine. He raised his voice, small though it must have sounded echoing off the damp stone walls that surrounded him, and made music. "Sometimes," he later recalled, "I sang songs like 'I Am a Child of God' and 'Everybody's Got to Have a Hero.' I knew that whoever found me would be my hero."[12]

At last, his prayers were answered. Searchers found him and carried him out, weak but alive. And everyone agreed that if that mine ever did hold any hidden treasure, it was Joshua himself.

What do you think really kept him alive? His desire to live, for sure. (Including his desire to chow down a big bag of French fries.) His ability to adapt to a world of complete darkness, with none of life's normal rhythms, not even a line between day and night. And his faith—in something higher, something larger, than himself. *I am a child of God,* he sang. And that faith gave him comfort as well as strength.

It's time to mention another tool for survival: a sense of humor. Which means it's time to mention Satchel Paige.

Satchel grew up in Mobile, Alabama, in the early 1900s, when many black people faced poverty and humiliation every single day. Satchel's family, with twelve kids, was extremely poor. On top of that, he kept getting into trouble. Once he was arrested for shoplifting and sent away to reform school. And he got into more fights than he could count.

But Satchel Paige loved two things, loved them intensely. One was playing baseball (though as a kid the only things he could find to throw were rocks). And the other was laughing. This fellow simply loved a good joke—especially if it made fun of him. And his ability to laugh helped him survive.

On the way to becoming a legendary baseball player—and the first African-American pitcher voted into the Hall of Fame—he faced lots of tough hurdles, starting with his childhood and continuing through the painful discrimination that kept him out of the major leagues until he was in his forties. But did he lose his sense of humor? No way. Just listen to how he described his own beginnings:

> It don't matter what some of those talkers say, I wasn't born six feet, three and a half inches tall, weighing a hundred and eighty pounds and wearing size fourteen shoes. And there wasn't a baseball in my hand, either. I was just a baby like any other baby born south of Government Street, down by the bay in Mobile. . . . I went around with the back of my shirt torn, a pair of dirty diapers or raggedy trousers covering me. Shoes? They was somewhere else. . . . Since I threw those rocks so straight, I guess it was just natural that I started firing a baseball.[13]

Such humor can be very powerful. For if you can laugh at your own predicaments, you can usually survive them. That's because humor gives you a little distance—a break—from your troubles. And that may be all you need to overcome them. After all, the word *levity*, which stems from the Latin word *lev-*

itas, has two meanings: One involves being funny, and the other, being lighter. And that connection isn't just a coincidence. By finding ways to laugh, you are also finding ways to lighten your load.

Satchel Paige knew that well. Through all his hardships, he lived by his motto: "Don't look back. Something might be gaining on you."[14]

Satchel's humor reminds me of someone else I admire, Abraham Lincoln. Now, no leader in our history has ever borne a greater weight than this humble man from Illinois. He tried to hold his nation together, win a brutal civil war, free the slaves from bondage, and at the same time foster a spirit of compassion for the defeated South. Add to this an unhappy family life, the death of a child, and an onslaught of criticism during his presidency.

How did he keep going through all this? Simple: He never forgot how to laugh. When someone accused Lincoln of being "two-faced," he quickly replied, "If I really did have another face, do you think I'd still wear this one?" And when he was criticized for not speaking often enough, he answered, "It is better to remain silent and be thought a fool, than to open your mouth and remove all doubt." Then he had only one thing to say about a rival who favored slavery: "He can compress the most words into the smallest ideas of any man I ever met."[15]

There you have it: Humor . . . and a load that feels a little bit lighter.

As Satchel Paige and Abraham Lincoln understood, survival isn't always about life or death for your body. Sometimes it's more about life or death for your soul. It can take just as much bravery, adaptability, and faith to survive what they did as it does to survive an avalanche. And it can take the same qualities to survive a bigoted mob, a violent home, or a tough neighborhood. In such situations, your challenge isn't to keep breathing, to fill your lungs with air. It's to fill your soul with hope, and the courage to face another day.

Nobody, I believe, ever showed more of this kind of heroism than Ruby Bridges. What a girl!

Ruby was just six years old, in New Orleans, when the national spotlight—and the whole civil rights movement—landed right on top of her. As she said in her marvelous autobiography, *Through My Eyes*: "It was 1960, and history . . . swept me up in a whirlwind. At the time, I knew little about the racial fears and hatred in Louisiana, where I was growing up."[16]

All that changed in a flash when Ruby became the first black child ever to enter an all-white school. Gripping her mother's hand, and flanked by federal marshals, she walked bravely up the school steps. An angry mob jeered at this little girl with a white ribbon in her hair, shouting taunts and hurling stones.[17] But Ruby kept right on walking . . . past the crowd, through the doors to her school, and onto the pages of American history.

Think about how she must have felt that day—scorned and taunted just because of the color of her skin. And think about the pressures on anyone who is a part of a minority, whether it's a minority of race or religion or lifestyle. If you've ever said no to cigarettes or drugs, declined to ride with a drunken driver, or stood up for someone being bullied, then you have experienced some of those pressures. And you know how intense they can be.

The most beautiful crystals on Earth, though, are formed in the harshest pressures. Chemically, a diamond is the same as a plain old lump of coal: Both are made from carbon. The difference is that a diamond has survived incredible heat and weight. It has grown stronger—and shines brighter—because of all it has survived.

RUBY BRIDGES

Just like Ruby Bridges.

And here's some good news. Ruby is part of a long parade of young people who have stood up against hatred and bigotry. Take, for example, the brave civil rights activists brought to life in Ellen Levine's classic, *Freedom's Children*. And the parade grows longer all the time, as two brave boys from Idaho showed recently.

Neto Villareal, who is Hispanic, and Andy Percifield, who is not, felt outraged by the racist insults that some of their fellow Marsing High School students hurled at Hispanics on the school's football team. So they swung into action. Neto boldly organized a boycott by athletes, while Andy drafted a new school policy condemning racial slurs. The result? A solid first step toward ending racism at their school.[18]

Heroes of this kind have another quality going for them: a clear sense of right and wrong. It's a kind of compass, really. A moral compass. One guided not by something as unreliable as peer pressure, but by something far more true—in this case, the principle that all people deserve respect. Without a compass of this kind, it's all too easy to get lost. With one, though, it's possible not just to survive, but to lead people in a better direction.

That's what a Thai girl named Prateep did. Born into an impoverished family, Prateep Ungsongtham Hata grew up in the most hideous slums of Bangkok. In those crumbling neighborhoods, disease, starvation, and crime are everywhere. There are no septic systems, no garbage bins, no hospitals, and no police officers. Just to live, Prateep was forced to work long hours as a child laborer, earning five baht (about twenty-five cents) a day, doing jobs such as scraping rust from the hulls of freight ships.

PRATEEP UNGSONGTHAM HATA
AND STUDENTS

One day, when she was thirteen, Prateep fell through some rotten planks near the harbor and gashed her leg. She lay there, bleeding, staring at her neighborhood. In that moment, she made up her mind to survive it—and help others do the same. And so she began to organize a school for the children of the slums. It took many years, but finally she established the Pattana Village Community

School, whose goal is to give kids basic education and health care.[19] Plus something else, even more precious: a touch of hope.

Now, most of us don't have to face the extreme poverty of Prateep's childhood. Or the bigotry of Ruby Bridges' neighbors. Or the loneliness of Joshua Dennis' abandoned mine. And yet every day we must face challenges of our own. They may be more ordinary—a tough day at school, a twisted ankle, or a bully on the bus—but they can be plenty demanding. And also helpful, for they can show us we have more inside ourselves than we might think.

Sometimes the struggles of everyday life can teach us much about surviving. That's what happened to me on a particularly sad day—the day my dad died. Our normally lively, bustling home was somber and quiet. And I felt numb inside. All I wanted to do was get through that day, and the days of grieving to come.

To survive.

My wife, our young kids, and I sat down at our kitchen table for supper. We passed around a bowl of cold spaghetti— cold because I'd come home late from seeing my dad for the last time. Then, without saying a word, the kids started telling stories about the grandpa they loved. Some were poignant, such as the last walk with him down to the creek on his ranch. Some were funny, such as the time he carved a hole in the bottom of a jack-o-lantern, put it on his head, and scared the living daylights out of my wife. And some were just plain wistful . . . such as his plan to build a tree house in the old cottonwood tree, something he never got to do.

Suddenly, I realized that my dad wasn't really as far away as

I'd thought. And that while I wouldn't stop missing him, I would someday stop grieving. For our memories of him were very much alive.

I'd like to end this chapter with a person who showed all the qualities of a survivor hero—and then some. Her name? Anne Frank.

When Nazi troops invaded Holland and started harassing, torturing, and murdering any Jews they could find, Anne's family and some friends—eight people—hid in the secret annex of a house in Amsterdam. When I visited that house myself a while ago, I couldn't believe that all those people had lived for more than two years in that cramped space. Or that they had lived with such constant fear.

Soldiers were everywhere, you see. As were paid informers. Even before she had moved to the secret annex, Anne had seen more than her share of brutality in her thirteen years—people carted off to die in gas chambers and slave camps, beaten by thugs, robbed of their dignity. And no one knew when or even if World War Two might end.

Yet Anne found a way to hope, sing, and pray all in one: in her diary. Toward the end of her long confinement, she wrote, "It's really a wonder that I haven't dropped all my ideals. . . . Yet, in spite of everything, I still believe that people are really good at heart."[20]

Good at heart. Think of what courage—and hope—it took to say that in the midst of her persecution!

Tragically, Anne Frank's family was betrayed to the Nazis just before the end of the war. Anne died of typhus in a concentration camp, barely one month before she would have been rescued by the Allies. She joined more than six million

Jews, including more than a million children, who died in the horror of the Holocaust.

And yet . . . in one way Anne did survive. Her diary, left behind on the floor of the secret annex when the Nazis captured her family, was later found by her father and published in 1947. Swiftly, it became an international best-seller. Translated into more than fifty languages, it has now become one of the most widely read books of all time. So her voice, frail but hopeful, lives on.

ANNE FRANK

Young people have confronted plenty of challenges on the hero's trail—and kept right on walking. Despite all the hardships they've faced, they haven't lost their footing, or their hopes. They have remembered how to sing in the face of troubles. And even how to laugh.

For such resilience under pressure, you could call them diamonds. Or better yet . . . call them survivors.

More Survivor Heroes . . .

Norvell Smith tried hard to stay out of trouble—no easy feat in her neighborhood, the violent south side of Chicago. Once she accidentally walked into a gang fight and a bullet barely missed her waist. Finally, Norvell decided that surviving meant more than dodging bullets. So she started speaking out against gangs and their destructive effects on kids. And

NORVELL SMITH AND FRIEND

her speeches made an impact—so much that her school became a model of safety. Now many more schools around Chicago have asked her to speak. Norvell's ability to survive has convinced others that they can do the same.[21]

Sokhoeun Chhunn

arrived in Rochester, Minnesota, as a Cambodian refugee when she was thirteen years old. Though she treasured her new freedom, at school she suffered racist insults and humiliation. Did she shrink away and hide? No, just the opposite. She organized a whole string of cultural events to introduce students to new lands

SOKHOEUN CHHUNN

and peoples. And more. She worked hard to create an annual leadership conference for high school students from all sorts of racial, ethnic, and religious backgrounds.[22]

Archie McNealy hails from Miami, Florida. His whole life has been a story of survival, from his difficult childhood to his dangerous part of town. Just getting to school each day in one piece—and avoiding drug dealers on the way—took all his street smarts and determination. But Archie didn't quit. And he did so well at school that he won a full scholarship to college at Florida A & M, where he plans to major in business.[23]

Liberty Franklin never knew her father, and her youth was rife with pain. This young woman of Everett, Washington, could easily have considered herself a victim. But that's just not how Liberty thinks. In sixth grade, she joined the local Boys & Girls Club, then she started working at different jobs, earning money to help her family. And she worked hard in school, too—graduating in 1999 at the very top of her class.[24]

Nathan Hale is well known as a great American patriot. But he was also a great survivor. This young man's life changed forever when fighting broke out in 1775 between the colonial militia and the British. He joined the militia himself, and became America's first spy. The dignity and devotion he showed inspired many people around him. And his final words still inspire today: "I only regret that I have but one life to lose for my country."[25]

Keema McAdoo, as an eighth-grader in Dorchester, Massachusetts, saw teen violence on the rise—right in her own neighborhood. Worried about her own safety and that of her sisters, she set up an after-school program to steer kids away from drugs and crime, and get them involved with basketball and a local recycling project. Her program worked so well that, before long, other schools in town asked her to do the same for them. For Keema, survival depended on building a safer neighborhood.[26]

Satchmo, whose name at birth was **Louis Armstrong,** became a phenomenal trumpeter and one of the greatest jazz musicians of the twentieth century. But his childhood was terribly hard. After his father abandoned them, Louis' family lived in poverty in a two-room house in New Orleans. Young Louis delivered coal to help buy food. One New Year's Eve, he celebrated by firing a pistol in the street— and found himself arrested and sent to the Colored Waifs Home for Boys. There, he learned a little music from the band director, and discovered that he loved to play the trumpet.

LOUIS ARMSTRONG

In a few years, Satchmo was dazzling audiences around the world. People think of him as a consummate musician . . . but he was also a consummate survivor.[27]

Our deepest fear is not that we are inadequate. Our deepest fear is that we are powerful beyond measure.

—Nelson Mandela

4 Hero Within

It hits me so fast, I can't explain how. Or why.

You and I, along with Herc, are camping at Blue Lake. Even for early spring, it's cold. So cold that icicles hang from tree limbs and snow still clings to the slopes. Earlier in the day, we ended our climb by skiing down the mountain on our backsides, spraying snow and howling like a pair of wild coyotes as we skidded through the pines.

Right before it happens, I am sitting outside our tent, trying to get my old camp stove to light.

"Hey," you call. "Elk!"

I look up from the sputtering old contraption to watch a whole herd step out of the trees and start to graze by the lake. They look shaggy with heavy coats of brown. And plenty hungry after a long winter! Herc growls at the bull in the lead. But when the big elk raises his antlered head and bellows back, the rest of the herd barely stirs. They just keep munching on blades of grass.

And Blue Lake—it's so much more than blue. In the late afternoon light, it glows like a sapphire, with hints of emeralds in its depths.

I turn back to the camp stove. Something has clogged one of the valves, so I turn the thing on its side and try to pry the valve open. No luck. It won't budge. Maybe I can melt whatever is blocking it? I strike a match, careful not to touch the fuel canister. Suddenly—

A blast of fire! Flames erupt from the stove, scorching my face. I shout and jump up. My head throbs. All I can smell is my own singed hair. And my eyelashes are stuck together. For a few seconds, I can't open my eyes.

Finally, I pull my eyelids open. But it's still dark! No lake, no Herc, no you. I can't see anything!

You help me down the trail. So does Herc, in his own way—nuzzling my legs, sniffing my hands. Even though I can't see where he is, I know he's near. And all the while, I'm wondering . . . Will I ever see Blue Lake again?

If you or I ever went blind, we would have to face lots of challenges outside ourselves: how to cross a busy street, how to make a meal, how to find a friend in a crowd. But every blind person I've known would agree that the biggest difficulties we'd face would lie within. Our fears, our self-doubts, our weaknesses of will—those are the greatest challenges of all.

Heroes within are people who have faced those sorts of challenges and triumphed. Of course, every kind of hero must wrestle with fears and doubts. As we've seen already, one aspect of being a hero on the spot, or a survivor hero, is overcoming those fears. Climbing those inner mountains. But how does that happen? To help us explore which qualities are crucial to inner heroism, this chapter will focus on people whose challenges must be faced primarily within.

Sometimes those qualities will be very similar to the ones we've found in other kinds of heroes. The courage it takes to overcome polio is not so different from the courage it takes to rescue someone who is drowning, or to survive a shipwreck. Sometimes, though, heroes within bring new qualities to the fore. Qualities of character, and also of the spirit.

Ready to start? Well, there's no better way to meet a pair of great athletes—two people who did more than climb their inner mountains. They ran to the top. And broke plenty of records on the way.

Wilma Rudolph was born the twentieth—that's right, twentieth—kid out of twenty-two, in a poor black family in Bethlehem, Tennessee. Her mother supported the family by washing other people's clothes and doing odd jobs—a very hard life. And to make matters worse, this was the 1940s, when racial discrimination kept black people out of the best jobs, restaurants, and schools, assaulting their dignity every day. So you could say that Wilma started off at the very bottom of the mountain.

But that wasn't all. As a toddler, she was struck by three ravaging diseases: scarlet fever, pneumonia, and worst of all, polio. Combined, they left Wilma with a twisted, weak leg—so weak that she had to drag around a heavy brace wherever she went. Everybody thought she'd never walk again.

Everybody, that is, but Wilma. She desperately wanted to walk—maybe even run—like other kids. More than that, she just *knew* somehow that she could do it. And so she practiced

every day in the front yard, working her bad leg until she sometimes collapsed from exhaustion and had to be carried back inside.

Finally, when she was ten years old, Wilma called to her mother to watch. Her mother stopped washing clothes and came over, not knowing what to expect. With a look of determination, Wilma tore off her brace and stood on her own. Then, all by herself, she walked across the yard and into her mother's open arms.

That wasn't all. Wilma started to run. She joined her high school track team. Pretty soon she won some races—as well as a scholar-

Photograph courtesy of Dover; Mark Kauffman/TimePix

WILMA RUDOLPH

ship to Tennessee State University. By the time she entered the 1960 Olympic Games, she had already broken several world records for speed. And she came home with three Olympic gold medals, more than any American woman had won in history.[28]

Wilma Rudolph, the kid with polio who was too weak to walk, had become the fastest woman in the world.

Ever heard of Glenn Cunningham? His hero's journey began on a cold Kansas morning in 1918, when Glenn was just eight years old. He and his brother had just run several miles that morning, since it was their turn to light the potbellied stove that heated their school, before the other kids arrived. Glenn's big brother had won their race, as usual. But Glenn didn't really mind. He just loved to run.

Suddenly the old stove exploded. Flames shot through the one-room schoolhouse before Glenn could even scream. When he woke up hours later, he found out that his brother had died in the blast. Glenn's own legs were so badly charred and burned that he couldn't move them at all. Not even his toes. Almost no muscle remained, and precious little skin. All Glenn could feel was pain. Deep, searing pain.

The doctor wanted to amputate both his legs. Better for the boy, he explained, since Glenn would surely never walk again. But Glenn howled in protest. Sure, what used to be his legs now looked more like dead branches, but they were still his! Finally Glenn prevailed.

For months, Glenn's parents came into his bedroom and sat beside him on the mattress, massaging what few threads of muscle remained. All the while, they hoped and prayed that one day he might walk again. Glenn prayed, too, but with more confidence than his parents. He *promised* them that he'd run again some day.

Slowly, very slowly, some feeling returned to his legs. Then he wiggled a toe, and bent his knee just a little. Finally came the day—almost one year after the explosion—when Glenn swung his feet over the side of his bed, put some weight on them, and tried to stand.

He rocked unsteadily, his whole body trembling. Then his legs buckled and he fell in a heap on the floor. For several minutes he just lay there. At last, he grabbed the bedpost and pulled himself up again. This time, he spread his legs farther apart. And this time, he stood.

The next day he took a few steps around his room. Then some more steps, walking faster. In time, he went outside to exercise. Just a few weeks later, he started to run.

Can you imagine how he felt? His legs, his own legs, could carry him again! He could lope, turn corners, and jump fences. He could feel the wind on his face, the ground under his feet. And though he still limped slightly, his speed improved. He entered a local race in the mile—and won. He kept running, winning trophies, and breaking records. He pushed harder and harder, beating his own best times. And finally, almost twenty years after that explosion that nearly cost him his legs, Glenn Cunningham achieved his greatest dream and set the world record in the mile.[29]

Both Wilma Rudolph and Glenn Cunningham proved the strength of their legs . . . as well as their determination. And also of something else, a quality that is especially important for heroes within.

Faith. In a higher power, first of all. In life itself. And also

in themselves: their own strength, their own potential to sur-
mount great obstacles. This many-layered faith—in God, life,
and themselves—gives such heroes great power.

How is this faith different from what we have seen before
in other heroes? In some ways, not at all. The faith of Joshua
Dennis, who kept singing in the darkness of that mine, or of
Anne Frank, who kept alive her hopes for her family—and for
humanity—isn't any less sturdy than the faith of these two athletes.

Yet there is one difference worth noting. The faith of heroes
within, while no stronger than that of other kinds of heroes, is
directed in a slightly different way—less at the outside world
and more at the hero's inner self. When you are trapped in a
mine, your ultimate hope is to be rescued. To be found by
searchers from beyond those walls of stone. When you are hid-
ing from Nazi soldiers who have invaded your country, your
ultimate hope is to be freed, to have your country liberated.
But when you are afflicted with polio or burned legs, your
rescue, your liberation, must come from inside yourself. And
so your ultimate hope lies within.

That's why Wilma's certainty that she would walk again
was so crucial. And why Glenn's promise to his parents that he
would run again was so meaningful. This kind of faith in yourself helps you do more than climb mountains. It helps you
move mountains.

Such faith has strengthened all sorts of people. Leaders,
poets, scientists, musicians, nurses, carpenters, humanitarians,
business executives, and astronauts have all faced tough challenges and prevailed. But only because they truly believed in
themselves.

Consider Stephen Hawking. As long as he could remember, he had wanted to be a great scientist or mathematician. Then suddenly, just after high school, all his hopes came crashing down. He took sick with a mysterious disease that confined him to bed with round-the-clock care. It turned out to be a rare neurological disorder that made it harder and harder for him to move. Even turning his head was too much for him.

On top of that, Stephen got pneumonia—so bad he couldn't breathe. A throat operation saved his life, but left him without any voice at all. Now the only way he could communicate was by blinking his eyes or wiggling his fingers. Things couldn't have been much worse for him. He had every reason to think of himself as a victim, to grow more bitter every day, to give up his dreams.

STEPHEN HAWKING

But not Stephen. He kept reading about science, especially the most recent developments in quantum physics. And he found himself a computerized voice synthesizer that could be fitted to his wheelchair. Now, just by moving his fingers, he could speak, ask questions, or discuss theories out loud. Through sheer determination, he continued his work, pushing ahead the frontiers of physics. He became a leading theorist on black holes, and his book *A Brief History of Time* turned into an international best-seller. And here is the best part: He now holds Isaac Newton's chair in mathematics at Cambridge University.[30]

Now, let's not forget that heroes of this kind, whose faith in themselves is so strong, also have their doubts. It's part of being human. Sometimes a person's doubts can last for years. Even a lifetime. But here is a marvelous thing about faith: It can coexist with doubt. It can even grow stronger in the face of doubt.

At some point, though, every hero within takes a step in the direction of confidence. That first step may be hesitant, or clumsy. It may also be spontaneous, without any real thought behind it. But it's a beginning—a start on the trail.

That's how it was for Joe Derat, Jr., of Dorchester, Massachusetts. You see, Joe stutters when he speaks. For years, his stuttering made him a target of brutal teasing in school. Anytime he spoke—calling across the playground, asking a question in class—he was laughed at, called names, or even beaten. As he put it, "The kids treated me like I was a piece of trash."[31]

JOE DERAT, JR.

That was unfair to Joe, and very painful. But the worst part was that he didn't know what to do about it. And yet . . . at some level he sensed that unless he stood up for him-self, nobody else would.

So one day in third grade, Joe did something he'd never done before.

Something courageous. "All the other kids were laughing at me. . . . I dried my eyes, went up to the front of the room, and said, 'I don't care what you think about me. The only thing that matters is what I think about myself.'"[32]

Joe's problems haven't totally disappeared, mind you. But in that moment he discovered that there is someone he can always rely on, someone with real inner strength. Someone named Joe.

People who triumph over difficult obstacles—whatever form those obstacles may take—often have something else going for them. A kind of attitude. Do you think Wilma Rudolph would have prevailed if she had thought of herself as just a victim, if she had focused more on her limits than her possibilities? No chance. She saw her weak leg as a challenge. And her life, for all its struggles, as a gift.

In short, she had a positive spirit.

It's a hard thing to define, positive spirit. But it's not about avoiding your troubles. Not at all! Being positive and being realistic can go hand in hand. In fact, the two qualities often strengthen each other, in the way that the two sides of a stepladder support each other's weight.

Positive spirit means, when you are climbing up a steep ridge, that you remember to celebrate how far you've come even as you consider how much farther you have to go. That you believe in the power of your skills, drive, and experience. And that you have confidence in life to show you the way if you try hard enough to find it. It means seeing opportunities along with obstacles, solutions along with problems.

And it can make all the difference in the world. Just ask Lauren Detrich and Fox Beyer.

Lauren's family and friends in Tulsa, Oklahoma, call her Lo. But they might as well call her *fighter*. When she was born with cystic fibrosis, a disease of the lungs and digestive system, the doctors gave her little chance to live past her teens. And practically no chance for a rewarding life.

For people with cystic fibrosis, something as simple as walking or tying their own shoes can be a huge challenge. Just to keep from being debilitated by her disease, Lauren takes great quantities of pills and spends three hours every day using special breathing equipment. In Lo's words, "Every breath of life is a prayer answered."[33]

Lo enjoys her life, though. She laughs easily and likes being with her friends. Perhaps that's one reason why she is now a teenager, and still going strong. And she isn't just waiting around, hoping someone will find a cure soon. She has become a top fund-raiser for cystic fibrosis research. Last year, after working hard to find sponsors, she joined a walkathon and raised nearly fifty thousand dollars. Then she organized a dance to raise even more.

Photograph courtesy of Doug Hole

LAUREN DETRICH

And you can bet that Lo was out there dancing with everyone else.

That same can-do attitude shines through Fox Beyer of Chatham, New Jersey. Born ten weeks early, he hung at the edge of death, with collapsed lungs and other problems—but still survived. Then came more bad news. Fox was diagnosed with cerebral palsy, which twisted his body and made every move a struggle. By the time he was five years old, for example, he had so much trouble walking that doctors needed to break both his legs, move the bones, and reset them just so Fox could get around.

But Fox had something else on his mind besides his problems. Baseball. He really wanted to play! And knew, somehow, that he could. So his dad set up a batting cage in their yard, and they practiced for hours hitting, catching, and pitching. Despite his ongoing pain, and several operations, Fox kept at it. By age twelve, he was accepted at Little League summer camp. In high school, he began as a relief pitcher, but soon joined the varsity and wound up pitching more innings than any other player on his team.[34]

I'd call that a home run. Wouldn't you?

Fox reminds me of another baseball player: Lou Gehrig, the legendary first baseman for the New York Yankees. Now, here was a fighter! After years of athletic feats, Lou developed a strange ailment that made him drop balls and stumble over his own feet. Doctors couldn't even diagnose it, let alone cure it. (It's now called Lou Gehrig's disease.) But he plugged on, game after game. Finally, the disease made it so hard for him to control his muscles that he could barely move around. He had to retire. Pale and weak, he addressed his thousands of fans at Yankee Stadium. "I may have been given a bad break," he declared for all to hear, "but I still consider myself the luckiest man on Earth."[35]

Luckiest? Now, how could he say that? After all his suffering, all his humiliation? Baseball was, after all, more than just his sport. It was his life.

Well, he could say that because he believed it. He knew that life had given him more than a ravaging disease. It had given him great gifts, as well: raw talent, many years of good health, and the chance to do something he really loved. Just because his time playing baseball had been rudely cut short, he wasn't about to forget all the great experiences he'd had. In other words, he chose to view his glass as half full instead of half empty. And the most remarkable thing about that positive spirit, which every hero within knows, is that when you focus on the fullness of the glass, you have already started to fill it even more.

My daughter, Denali, once gave me a great example of that sort of attitude. She was only four years old, but she couldn't have said it better.

I had taken her with me on a day of hiking in the high country (which was, for her, a day of bouncing around on my back). Both of us had loved it—a trail through aspen groves, a crystalline lake, and a meadow filled with wildflowers. We had discovered a waterfall, surprised a pair of foxes, and eaten a week's worth of chocolate. And when we returned home and I tried to put her to bed, she howled in protest. Tired as she was, she just didn't want that day to end.

"This is the most fungood day of my life," she said, throwing off her wool blanket.

"I know." Gently, I tucked her in again. "But now you need some sleep."

"I'll be so *sad* when it's midnight," she went on. "Then the day is really, really over."

"Yes, yes, we'll both be sad. Now sleep."

I got up to leave. Then, just as I was about to turn out her bedroom light, she suddenly sat up. "Daddy!" she cried, her eyes as round as full moons.

"What now?" I grumbled.

She gazed at me. "You know what midnight really means?"

I rolled my eyes. "If I tell you, will you finally go to sleep?" Seeing her nod, I answered, "It means the end of your fun-good day."

She shook her head. "No, something else." She smiled ever so slightly. "It means the start of *another* day."

Now, many times since that night, her words have come back to me. Usually when I've felt sad or hopeless—like it was midnight in my life. And then I've heard that small voice again, reminding me it's just the start of another day.

All the heroic people we've met in this chapter would agree that difficult times are painful, but they do have one virtue: They help us grow. Why is that? Because in our struggles we dig deep into ourselves, into our hidden reserves of strength and spirit. Just as heat can strengthen steel, hardship can strengthen people.

That has happened to many of our world's most remarkable leaders. Think of Abraham Lincoln, Nelson Mandela, Eleanor Roosevelt, Mohandas Gandhi, Mother Teresa, Winston Churchill, and so many others. And, of course, our greatest religious leaders—Jesus Christ, Moses, Buddha, Confucius, Mohammed—have all suffered, and grown even stronger through the experience.

One example you may not have heard about was a boy named Sundiata. Born in West Africa in the thirteenth century, Sundiata was weak and sickly. He couldn't even stand or walk, his legs were so frail. The only way he could get around the dusty streets of his village was to drag himself by his arms. Then, to everyone's surprise, a seer prophesied that Sundiata would someday become a powerful king who would rule like a lion.

Suddenly he had jealous enemies everywhere. Some of them captured his mother and tortured her before she finally escaped. When Sundiata found out, he vowed to protect her. So he called on every particle of strength inside himself, and forced himself to walk with a cane. To save his family and followers from attack, this boy who for years couldn't even stand on his own led them on a long trek to safety. It was said that only the sun in the heavens was more powerful than Sundiata's will.

Years later, Sundiata returned to his homeland and defeated his rivals in a great battle. He became the ruler of a new nation called Mali. And his people, remembering the prophecy, dubbed him "The Hungering Lion."[36]

Now, before closing this chapter I would like to salute one girl whose very name symbolizes the hero within. She combined all the qualities we have seen—courage, faith, and positive spirit—with a relentless desire to know and explore the world around her.

I speak of Helen Keller. This girl was born in a small town in Alabama before the start of the twentieth century. When she was just nineteen months old, Helen fell sick with a high fever. Though she lived, she was left both deaf and blind. Suddenly she was stuck in a world with no light and no sound—the ultimate solitary confinement. Often, she raged at her prison, screaming and kicking and breaking things around her. Wouldn't you? But this was a prison she couldn't escape.

Then one day in her seventh year, the walls around her cracked. Just a little . . . but enough to let in some light. Her teacher, Anne Sullivan, had tried for several weeks to teach Helen sign language so they could communicate. But every attempt had failed. And on this day they had failed again. Dejected, they went outside together. As Helen recounts in her autobiography:

> Someone was drawing water, and my teacher placed my hand under the spout. As the cool stream gushed over one hand, she spelled into the other the word *water*, first slowly, then rapidly. I stood still, my whole attention fixed upon the motions of her fingers. Suddenly I felt a misty consciousness . . . and somehow the mystery of language was revealed to me. I knew that "w-a-t-e-r" meant the wonderful cool something that was flowing over my hand. That living word awakened my soul, gave it light, hope, joy, set it free![37]

Helen was on her way. She quickly learned to speak sign language and read Braille. Ultimately she attended Radcliffe College and became a highly acclaimed author who touched millions of people through her writings. Confined to her prison no more, this girl who had once been denied the power of words could now speak loud and clear. She had won that power back—and used it to inspire others around the world.

Now you know another group of trail guides. They are a diverse lot, as always, but in every case their trails lead under their skin and into their deepest selves. Their struggles are shaped by the forces of attitude, belief, and spirit. And they remind us all just how powerful those forces can be.

For they are heroes within.

More Heroes Within . . .

Terry Fox was just eighteen years old when he developed cancer in his right leg—so severe that it had to be amputated above the knee. As much as he missed having two good legs, this young man from Winnipeg, Manitoba, made up his mind to run again. Fitted with an artificial leg, he began to train. And he hatched the idea of raising money for cancer research by running all the way across Canada. On April 12, 1980, Terry dipped his artificial foot into the Atlantic Ocean and set off. By September 1, he had run 3,339 miles—but had to stop because his cancer had reappeared, this time in his lungs. Though he didn't complete the run and died a short time later, Terry did achieve his primary goal: His Marathon of Hope raised more than $24 million for the fight against cancer.[38] As Terry himself put it: "Dreams are made if people try."[39]

Seth Ginsberg, in 1995, was thirteen and a sprinter on his school's track team in Spring Valley, New York, when he started feeling sharp pains in his joints. Growing pains? No—

arthritis. He discovered he was one of three hundred thousand youngsters with the disease. "Even with medicine, it's hard," he explained. "In the mornings my joints are stiff. Often I have to crawl to the bathroom."[40] But Seth didn't give in. He continued to work hard in school. And he still had enough energy to volunteer at his local chapter of the Arthritis Foundation. For Seth had also discovered just how much strength he had down inside.

Carol Heiss loved to skate. At age ten her athletic career looked bright—until she crashed into another skater on the ice. The other girl's blade sliced Carol's left leg so badly that she feared she'd never skate again. For a while she couldn't even bear to put on her skates, let alone perform acrobatic leaps and spins. But she persisted, and in time conquered her fears. Nearly a decade later, in 1956, Carol skated her way to a world championship. And her main rival in that event, the defending world champion, was **Tenley Albright**—an equally courageous athlete who had fought her way back from childhood polio.[41]

Sadako Sasaki showed such courage during her brief life in Japan that she inspired a worldwide following. Stricken with leukemia, a result of bomb radiation from World War Two, Sadako wished for world peace—and did her best to make that wish come true. Recalling an ancient Japanese tradition that someone who makes one thousand origami paper cranes will have any wish granted, she started folding cranes. When, at age ten, she finally died, she had finished 634 of them. So her schoolmates made 356 more to total one thousand. Soon people all over Japan were making more cranes in her honor. And more: They created the Hiroshima Peace Park, with a statue of Sadako holding a golden crane. Today, people from all over the world come to the park to echo this girl's wish for lasting peace.[42]

Lance Armstrong is well known as a world champion cyclist, winner of the Tour de France and dozens of other races. You may also know that he won his first major competition when he was just thirteen years old. But did you know that, in 1996, just after he'd become the top-ranked cyclist in the world, Lance developed cancer? It had spread to his lungs and brain, making his chances to survive fifty-fifty at best. Yet he didn't give up. Right after chemotherapy, he went back to training and pushed himself harder than ever. Before long, he was a leading competitor again. And in 2001 he won a stunning third straight victory at the Tour de France.[43]

Photograph courtesy of Charles Platiau Reuters/Getty Images

LANCE ARMSTRONG

Mattie Stepanek was born with a severe form of muscular dystrophy that makes him need a ventilator, oxygen tanks, and constant care. Three of his siblings died from the same condition. But this young man's spirit is made from sturdy stuff. Since the age of three, he has written thoughtful, creative, and funny poems, many of which have been published. He brims with gratitude for life, bright colors, and his loving fam-

MATTIE STEPANEK

ily. When he grows up, he declares, he wants to be "a daddy, a writer, a public speaker, and a peacemaker."[44] He is *already* a hero.

Samuel Long had a tough beginning: Seizures, comas, and constant trips to the hospital dominated his childhood in Missouri. But Sam wanted more. Though he was deaf, he saw someone break dancing and wanted to do it. So he signed up for a class, telling no one he couldn't hear. And mastered all the moves! Then he chose to join the Boy Scouts—and kept on trying to join even after he was turned down. Eventually he won acceptance, as well as a First Class rank. Next Sam set his sights even higher, clocking hundreds of hours as a volunteer teaching disabled kids how to walk, swim, or

SAMUEL LONG

use sign language. And in 1990, he coached a Special Olympics team for his high school.[45]

Geerat Vermeij hated being blind as a child in the Netherlands. As he wrote in his autobiography, "I was gripped with a sense of entrapment in a world of loneliness and fear."[46] Even so, he pursued his passion for science. Shells, in particular, fascinated him—and he discovered that with his fingers he could "see" things that other people missed. And see them well! Today he is one of the world's top authorities on mollusks, and a leading evolutionary biologist.

Itzhak Perlman is today a highly acclaimed musician who performs throughout the world. As a child in Israel, though, he was the son of a barber—and a boy with severe polio. But that disability didn't stop him from following his passion for music. And millions today are glad of that! For he is now a virtuoso violinist of the first rank. And something more: He is living testimony to the power of the human spirit.[47]

ITZHAK PERLMAN

Photograph courtesy of Getty Images

You must be the change you wish to see in the world.
—Mohandas Gandhi

⑤ Hero to Others Near and Far

Herc!"

The dog's shaggy shape crashes into the underbrush by the trail. Torn leaves spray into the air. All I can see is his tail, sticking out of the branches. He gives a gruff bark at the squirrel he's chasing and plunges deeper. Then he's gone—tail and all.

I shake my head and smile. And start walking again, knowing that he'll follow when he's ready. My boots crunch on aspen leaves that have landed on the trail like thousands of yellow butterflies. The air is crisp. On the summits beyond the trees, I can see the first traces of snow. As I round the bend, the trail opens onto a meadow. And there, by the blue columbines at the meadow's edge, is the hut.

Our hut. Built by you and me over the summer. Tons of work, for sure. But just look at it now! The lichen-spotted stones that we hauled and chipped and fit into walls. The fallen firs we split into beams for the roof. And of course, that cursed chimney that fell in on us so many times before we made it sturdy enough for mountain storms.

I sniff the air. Mixing with the smell of wood smoke is something rich. Shaggy-mane mushrooms? I stride across the meadow and open the door.

You look up from tending the fire. "Hey, it's about time," you say. "The work's all done and the stew is ready."

"That's called perfect timing." I set my pack on the floor. "Comes from years of practice."

You pull over a pair of stools and grin at me. "Guess you deserve it, after all the stuff you taught me this summer."

We pour bowls of thick mushroom stew, then sit together by the fire, watching it crackle. In time, you turn back to me. "Hard to believe we built this whole place ourselves."

"Sure is! And now it's part of the park system, open to any hikers who might need shelter."

You take a sip of stew. "Does it ever bother you that it's not just ours? I mean, after all that work? We'll never get to meet most of the people who stay here. Never hear their stories. Or even their thanks."

I watch the flames. "They'll be thanking us all the same."

You nod, firelight glowing in your eyes. "I guess we're all walking the same trail."

When we think of life as a hike, a journey, we can often feel alone. After all, it takes courage just to start down life's trail, and to keep on walking. It takes more courage to be responsible for our choices, for who we are, and for the life we create. And it takes even more to make those choices—those footsteps—heroic ones.

But let's not forget how many aspects of this journey we share with others. Not just with every person alive today, but with all those who have gone before and are yet to be born. Our fellow hikers give us company on the journey, and sometimes help along the way. For we are all walking the same trail.

In earlier chapters, we've met many heroes who helped people. Some have been heroes on the spot, whose bravery saved lives. Some have been survivor heroes or heroes within, whose examples inspired others. Now . . . let's meet some heroes of another kind, people who consciously *set out* to help others. That was their goal from the start—to enrich their community, to make a difference to their world.

They are heroes to others near and far. And as diverse as these people are, they all understand one thing: We are all connected to one another. Across cultures, genders, times, distances, and beliefs. We are all made of the same stuff . . . something part clay, and part stardust.

Black Elk, the great wise man of the Oglala Sioux, knew this. He crafted a famous prayer that celebrates our connection to one another, and to the living Earth that supports us: "Hear me, four quarters of the world—a relative I am! Give me the strength to walk the soft Earth, a relative to all that is."[48]

Believe it or not, there is actually a theory of modern

physics about this kind of connectedness. It's called *the butterfly effect*. Why that name? Well, the theory states that everything in the universe is linked, beyond whatever we can see. These invisible links stretch across vast reaches of time and space. And they are so strong that even something very small— as small as a butterfly—could start a chain reaction that ultimately makes a huge difference. So even the slightest flutter of a butterfly's wings somewhere on this planet could actually, over time, change the course of the stars.

Just think about that. If we are all so closely connected, then every single one of us could make a difference. A small one, perhaps, but a difference nonetheless. That is the hallmark of this kind of hero.

Nobody exemplifies this better than Prometheus, legendary hero of the ancient Greeks. They told of a time, long ago, when fire belonged just to the gods. Nobody else. And the king of the gods, Zeus himself, had commanded that it should stay that way forever.

Prometheus, however, disagreed. He watched people suffering without fire—babies freezing to death on wintry nights, families never sharing a hot meal or even a hearth to warm their hands. And his heart filled with sympathy. So one day he made up his mind to help.

Secretly, Prometheus tied a stalk of fennel to the chariot of Apollo. As the god's chariot rode near the sun, the stalk caught fire. Prometheus snatched up the burning stalk, brought it down to the world, and lit a pile of brush. It burst into flames. People came running over, gazing in awe. They felt the fire's warmth and sensed its power. At long last fire, the prize of the gods, belonged to all.

People everywhere cheered. But not Zeus the Thunderer! He was so angry that he captured Prometheus, chained him to a cliff, and commanded a great eagle to gnaw forever on his liver. Now Prometheus would writhe in agony for all time. Serious punishment, don't you agree? So the heroism of Prometheus really goes beyond his act of generosity and courage and includes his willingness to suffer for others. (Don't think the Greeks were completely heartless, though. In another myth, they ended his torture by having a different hero, Hercules, finally come to his rescue.)

Now, you can see how the heroism of Prometheus involved a conscious choice. Should he try to help all of humanity and give them fire, even if it meant bringing the wrath of Zeus down on his head? Or should he just play it safe? Maybe he could find some other, less risky way to help people. This sort of choice is never easy.

It's just this sort of choice, though, that defines heroes to others near and far. Like other people, they make choices based on their own personal values. But they must also take into account the high stakes involved, both for themselves and for society. Sometimes, doing what's right also means facing great danger. But heroes like Prometheus usually just look that danger in the eye and say, *Bring it on*.

Take the case of Teresa Prekerowa. Like everyone else, she felt helpless when, in 1939, German tanks rolled into Poland. Even worse, the invasion soon took a huge toll on her family. One of her brothers was captured and killed by the Nazis, and another was taken to a concentration camp. So it took a great deal of courage for this teenager to do what she did one night—to help a fellow human being.

Though Teresa's family was not Jewish, they lived in Warsaw not far from the ghetto where Jews had been forced to live. One night on her way home from school, Teresa heard something that made her stop. "It was a little girl who was crying . . . I think maybe she was three or four years old. She was wearing very, very poor clothes. And I looked at her, and saw she was Jewish."[49] Teresa hesitated, wondering what to do. If anybody saw her with the girl it could be extremely dangerous for her whole family. As she put it: "People who got caught helping Jews didn't come back home."[50]

She had plenty of reasons to keep walking, of course. She didn't know the Jewish girl at all. And besides, Teresa's family had more than enough troubles already. But how could she possibly leave this young girl all alone and unprotected? After a long moment of thought, Teresa took her by the hand, led her home, and gave her a meal and a bath. Then, in the dead of night, she smuggled the girl into a nearby convent, where the nuns agreed to keep her safe.

Teresa knew she couldn't save her whole country from the Nazis. But she could, at least, save one person. And that's just what she did.

History gives us many more examples of such heroism. Back in the 1820s, for instance, a Quaker boy in Indiana named Allen Jay cleverly used his parents' peach trees and cornfields to hide runaway slaves, then helped them find their way to safety.[51] And who could forget all the brave young people who joined in the civil rights movement in the 1950s and '60s? Nearly one thousand children joined Martin Luther King, Jr., in his march for freedom in Birmingham, Alabama, in 1963. Almost six hundred of those kids were arrested and thrown into jail. Some were badly beaten. But they never stopped singing and supporting one another. And as soon as they got out of jail, they went right back to work for the cause.[52]

Even after their victories, these civil rights activists didn't stop. They set about teaching the next generation about freedom. Gwendolyn Patton's family joined in the Montgomery, Alabama, bus boycott in 1955, when nearly fifty thousand black people stayed off the city's buses to protest the humiliating segregation that made black people ride in the back and give up their seats to anyone who was white. And in 1956, the boycotters won in court. So when Gwendolyn saw her mother board a bus and sit all the way in the back, she asked why. "Darling," came the reply, "the bus boycott was not about sitting next to white people. It was about sitting anywhere you please."[53]

Acts of heroism are like pebbles thrown into a pond. By itself, each pebble is very small. Yet the ripples it makes will spread farther and farther, becoming very large indeed, touching many faraway shores. And so, by setting fire to one thin stalk of fennel, our friend Prometheus gave a hearth fire to every home and a hot meal to every person, for all time. In the same way, by saving one girl's life, Teresa Prekerowa made it possible for that girl to grow up and help other people. And by stopping segregated buses in one city, civil rights activists started ripples that eventually touched every city and town in America.

All this makes me wonder whether the butterfly effect isn't just a theory about physics, after all. Perhaps . . . it's really a theory about life. Just one act of kindness or generosity can make a huge impact—whether on thousands of people nearby, or on one person thousands of miles away.

Just ask Rashad Williams of San Francisco. When he heard about the terrible shooting at Columbine High School in Colorado, Rashad couldn't get over what had happened to one student, Lance Kirklin. Just like Rashad, Lance had always loved to run. But in the shooting, he had been badly wounded in the chest, face, and leg—so badly he couldn't even walk, let alone run. On top of that, Lance didn't have the medical insurance to pay for the surgery he needed on his leg.

Rashad decided that it made no difference that he lived in another state and had different color skin than Lance. He just wanted to help. He signed up for a seven-mile race that would take place in San Francisco just one week later. During that week, he worked relentlessly to find sponsors who would donate money for Lance's surgery. And by the time he crossed the finish line, Rashad had raised nearly forty thousand dollars!

A grateful Lance had this to say about Rashad: "He's a great young man with a big heart. It means a lot to me that he did this for a complete stranger."[54] But even strangers, as Rashad knows, are really connected.

Michael Munds, too, knows about connections. Though he was born with disfiguring Treacher Collins syndrome, this young man from Denver, Colorado, has never dwelled on his own misfortune. Instead, he just loves to help others. When Michael was just six years old, he heard about the 1995 bombing of the federal building in Oklahoma City. Shocked by this terrible crime, he wanted to do something about it. So he made up his mind to raise money to help the families of the victims. Working hard, this six-year-old organized a bowling competition that netted over thirty-seven thousand dollars for those families.[55]

And he hasn't stopped there. Since then he has raised money for flood victims, burn victims, and others. Says Michael: "I believe that everyone can make a difference, no matter who you are, how old you are, or even what you look like."[56]

MICHAEL MUNDS

The connective tissue that binds all people together was seen everywhere after the September 11, 2001, terrorist attacks. You have heard many stories of heroism, I'm sure, ranging from brave police officers and firefighters to selfless emergency and medical workers. But you may not have heard about Julia DeVita and Caroline White, a pair of nine-year-olds from Charlotte, North Carolina.

When these two girls heard about the tragedy at the World Trade Center—where Julia's cousin, Jonathan Cappello, worked along with thousands of others—they wanted to help. But how? They were only kids, after all, and they lived a long way from New York City.

Remembering their past success at selling cookies and cold drinks to their neighbors, Julia and Caroline set up a new curbside stand. Only this time, all the proceeds went to the Red Cross. In just two days, they managed to raise over two thousand dollars. One man put a hundred dollars into their pickle jar. And kids at school stopped the girls in the hallways to give them even more money.[57]

In the same spirit, shortly after September 11, the children of Columbia, South Carolina, started collecting pennies wherever they could—at football games, bake sales, and other

JULIA DEVITA, CAROLINE WHITE, AND FRIENDS

events. Their goal? To buy a new fire truck for New York City.

It all began when Nancy Turner, principal of the White Knoll Middle School, discovered that, over one hundred years before, New York firefighters had donated a fire truck to Columbia after its devastation in the Civil War. Inspired by this long-ago gift, young people all over the city went to work. Soon civic leaders and others around the state joined in. Within two months, they had raised most of the three hundred fifty thousand dollars needed to buy a new fire truck.[58]

Wonderful as they are, these acts of generosity and hard work cannot erase the pain of such a great tragedy. Nothing, I am afraid, can do that. But they can add new, positive ripples

The Hero's Trail

to the pond we all share—ripples that could grow over time into wide-ranging waves.

Faced with a tragedy of their own, that's exactly what Valerie Edwards and Erin Scheide did. Valerie, a Maryland sixth-grader, was riding in a van in 1993 with her friend, Annie Davis. All of a sudden, a pickup truck plowed right into them, sending both girls to the hospital. Annie later died from her injuries.

Then came more bad news. Even though the pickup truck's driver may have been drinking, a loophole in Maryland law allowed him to avoid taking a blood alcohol test, so it was much harder to punish him for drunk driving. Valerie was outraged. Together with another courageous sixth-grader, Erin Scheide, and a helpful teacher, Diane Bragdon, they decided to do something about the problem. "It seemed that the laws were protecting the drunken drivers instead of the victims," explained Valerie. "We were determined to change that."[59]

And they did. They organized a group called For the Love of Annie, which made hundreds of information packets about the flawed law. They wrote to state legislators, then visited them personally and testified at hearing after hearing. Finally,

VALERIE EDWARDS AND
ERIN SCHEIDE

in 1994, a new, tougher law against drunk driving passed the Maryland legislature by unanimous vote. Maybe now others would be spared such tragedy . . . all for the love of Annie.

Today, many young people understand that we're connected not just to other people—but to other living creatures. And that we have a responsibility to God and ourselves to protect those creatures, to be good stewards of the planet. For all of us are part of God's creation. And all of us share the same home.

Andrew Holleman took this idea—and acted on it. Most of his life, this twelve-year-old from Chelmsford, Massachusetts, had hiked in a deep forest near his home. The trees were very beautiful—as was the wetland they sheltered. Then in 1987 he found out that the forest was going to be leveled by bulldozers for a new development. Before long, all those trees, plus the animals and birds who lived in them, would be destroyed.

Andrew plunged into researching what this would really mean to his community. He discovered that the sewage from

ANDREW
HOLLEMAN

the proposed development could possibly contaminate his town's drinking water. On top of that, he found that rare wood turtles and great blue herons, both endangered species, lived there. So he took his case to the town's zoning board. It took ten months, and dozens of meetings, but this determined lad finally won: The board voted to stop development in the forest.[60]

The second-grade class at Vidya Elementary School in Petaluma, California, also decided to help their fellow creatures. When the students learned from their teacher, Diana Lightman, that thousands of African elephants were being killed each year by poachers and tusk hunters, and that before long the whole species could be extinct, they took action. These kids formed a club called Friends of Wild Life (FOWL, for short). They held bake sales, sold T-shirts, and gave speeches to raise money, which they sent to conservation workers in Africa. What's more, they wrote over one thousand letters to officials in Washington, D.C., urging them to support a total ban on ivory from elephant tusks.

Guess what? In 1989, all their hard work finally paid off. The ban on elephant ivory was enacted into law.[61] And thousands of elephants now have a better chance to survive.

What those second-graders accomplished emphasizes that heroes have no size requirements. Even very small kids could help save the largest land animal on Earth! It reminds me of Aesop's fable about the tiny mouse who saved the life of a great lion. Not by using some powerful weapon, mind you, but just by chewing through the ropes that held the lion prisoner. In the same way, people who care enough and use whatever skills they have can make a great difference—even if their challenge seems much larger than themselves.

We have seen generosity and compassion aplenty in this chapter. Heroes to others near and far, fueled by their desire to do what's right, enrich the lives of many others—and their own, as well. For in the same way the ripples in a pond often bounce off the shore and return, every gift comes back to the giver. As my mother used to say, paraphrasing the Talmud,

"Whatever you take, you will someday lose. But whatever you give, you will always have."

Even so, it's important to remember that this kind of heroism doesn't come easily. It often involves real hardship. And real sacrifice. Prometheus proved that—and so did our final two heroes, one from Asia and one from North America.

In 1982, a boy named Iqbal Masih was born in a poor village in Pakistan. At the time, no one could have guessed how much suffering this boy would experience—or how much good he would accomplish.

From an early age, Iqbal loved sports. All kinds. He even dreamed of being a professional athlete someday. But those dreams suddenly ended when he was sold into slavery. And what was the price for Iqbal? Eight hundred rupees, or about sixteen dollars.

Even today, children in some parts of the world are sold as "bonded laborers"—a kind of slave. They are forced to work grueling hours with practically no food, fresh air, or pay. That's what happened to Iqbal. He was taken to a carpet factory, chained to a loom, and made to pull threads back and forth sixteen hours a day. It was exhausting, repetitive work. But if he ever complained, he was beaten. Sometimes his mouth was sealed shut with tape to keep him from talking.

Nothing, though, could stop Iqbal from thinking. About freedom—for himself and for the other children who were forced to work this way. He knew that there were laws in Pakistan against child slavery, even if they weren't always enforced. Maybe he could find some way to help.

One day, when his chains were released to let him sleep, Iqbal climbed over the factory fence and escaped. He ran to the local police station. Instead of helping him, though, they hauled him back to the factory. There, supervisors beat him, just to make sure he'd never try such a thing again.

But they didn't know Iqbal. He did escape again—and this time he found help. A Pakistani group devoted to freeing bonded laborers bought his release. At long last, Iqbal was free!

If he was ever tempted to give up on his goal of aiding other children, he never showed it. Iqbal went right to work, speaking out against bonded labor and urging stronger laws. Once he even managed to sneak into a carpet factory, pretending he was a worker. While inside, he gathered so much evidence of slavery, terrible conditions, beatings, and malnutrition, that his report caused a public outcry. The police were forced to raid the factory and free over three hundred halfstarved children.

Not long afterward, when Iqbal was twelve years old, his

IQBAL MASIH

life ended abruptly. He was riding his bicycle across a field when an unknown assassin fired a shotgun. Struck in the chest, Iqbal died within minutes. Over the next several days, thousands of Pakistanis filled the streets to mourn his loss.

And yet his work lives on. All over the world, people gathered to honor his memory, and to call for the end of bonded labor. At one school in Quincy, Massachusetts, the kids created a Web site that raised almost two hundred thousand dollars in donations to fund the Iqbal Masih Education Center in Pakistan. And a Canadian boy, Craig Kielburger, started an international group called Free the Children, dedicated to ending child slavery once and for all.[62]

"It takes a village to raise a child." That's an old African proverb about the connection between people of all ages. And very few people have shown the truth of that proverb better than Ryan Hreljac.

As a first-grade student at Holy Cross Catholic School in Kemptville, Ontario, Ryan was stunned to learn from his teacher that thousands of African children die every year just because they have no clean water. It didn't matter that he'd never met those children, or that they lived thousands of miles away. They were children—just like Ryan himself.

So this intrepid six-year-old took action. Told that one African well would cost seventy dollars, Ryan started doing extra chores around the house. Now, seventy dollars is a lot of money for someone so young to earn, but that didn't stop him. He vacuumed floors, washed windows, and more. Finally, he had the money. He proudly carried his jar of coins to an African relief agency.

Then he learned some bad news. His numbers were wrong!

A water well really cost two thousand dollars. He had earned only a small fraction of the total.

Undaunted, Ryan went right back to work. It took him many months—and lots of window spray—but at last he had the full amount. And thanks to him, a village in Uganda had its first clean well. "I keep telling people," says Ryan, "that if you really work hard and you really want something, you can do anything. My mom and dad didn't believe me before, but they sure do now."[63]

To Ryan's surprise, the ripples he had started came back to him. A generous neighbor was so impressed with his work that he gave Ryan a gift—plane tickets for him and his parents to visit Uganda. When Ryan arrived at the village, everyone turned out to welcome him. Finally, the children of the village led him over to the new well. And there he saw, inscribed on its base, the words *Ryan's Well*.[64]

All the young heroes we have met in this chapter have proved that their lives are linked to others. Empowered by

RYAN HRELJAC AND FRIENDS

their generosity, bravery, and sense of what's right, they have made a real difference to the world. And if you ever asked them why they took such risks and gave so much of themselves, they would tell you the answer is simple: We are connected to others near and far.

Because we're all walking the same trail.

More Heroes to Others Near and Far . . .

Grace Sanders couldn't believe the devastation when a 1998 tornado blasted through her hometown of Nashville, Tennessee. More than twenty thousand trees had been destroyed. So for her sixteenth birthday party, Grace asked her friends to bring no presents—but to bring some old clothes and a shovel instead. Over the course of that day, they planted nine healthy trees, with the help of ReLeaf Nashville, a nonprofit group. Grace described the day this way: "It gave us a good, warm feeling inside. And it was fun. It wasn't your normal birthday party."[65]

Justin Lebo from Paterson, New Jersey, loved to zip around town on his bicycle. And to tinker with the gears and brakes. When he realized how much riding his bike helped him enjoy the world, he decided to share that joy with others. So he started taking apart battered old bicycles, reassembling them, and giving the restored bikes to homeless and sick children. As word of his project spread, people from all over the area responded by donating old bikes. Over time, Justin has rebuilt and given away almost two hundred bikes.[66]

Jane Goodall enjoyed Tarzan stories when she was ten, so much that she longed to live with the animals of Africa and help protect them. Her wish came true: She has been studying chimpanzees for over forty years, and is now the world's leading expert on their society and communication. And that's not all. Jane Goodall has turned her energy to helping save other species—and, in the process, our planet. She formed Roots and Shoots, a worldwide network of young people who are concerned about the environment. "You, as an individual, can make a difference every day of your life," Jane declared. "And you can choose what sort of difference you want to make."[67]

Fernando Pantojas, age seventeen, made a tough choice—for himself and his community. Fed up with the power of gangs and drug peddlers in his tough Chicago neighborhood, he started counseling kids daily at the General Robert E. Wood Boys & Girls Club. He also organized projects aimed at building the kids' self-esteem so they wouldn't be drawn to gangs. "I try to be a positive influence," he explained. "One person can't save everyone, but I think I've helped some."[68]

Alexander Graham Bell is famous as the inventor of the telephone. But did you know that he started inventing things to help people when he was just a teenager? At age sixteen, he built a model of a human head that could actually speak, so he could find some way to combat his mother's deafness.[69] Eventually, his ingenuity led him to create the telephone. And just think of all the ripples that have flowed from that one invention: It's made possible the Internet, fiber optics, satellite communication, and more. And the ripples are still expanding.

Nkosi Johnson was born in Johannesburg, South Africa, with the virus that causes AIDS. When a public primary school refused to admit him, this spunky boy fought back and was finally allowed to enter school. Still, he faced teasing and isolation almost every day. Then Nkosi started giving speeches and interviews about the struggles of AIDS sufferers, in a country where ten percent—over four million people—are HIV positive. And people everywhere started listening. In 2001, at age twelve, Nkosi finally succumbed to the disease—but not before he had done a great deal to raise AIDS awareness throughout Africa.[70]

NKOSI JOHNSON

Andres Albeiro Luna, age five, is doing his part. Along with other Colombians, Andres is an active member of

Los Herederos del Planeta—
Inheritors of the Planet—whose
purpose is to devise better ways
to farm while also helping local
forests return to their natural
strength. Andres and his friends
have been working hard to de-
velop new organic farming tech-
niques, focusing on crops that
grow better because of the sur-
rounding wilderness. Farmers
are better off . . . and so is
Mother Earth.[71]

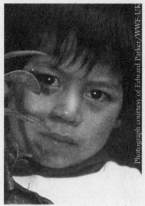

ANDRES ALBEIRO
LUNA

Michaella Gallina decided that all the fun she had
working with horses through her local 4-H club should be
shared. Especially by
kids who couldn't
move around as easily
as she could. So this
girl from Pueblo, Col-
orado, took the lead
in organizing an "Ex-
ceptional Rodeo" in
2000 for disabled chil-
dren, which included
"bucking broncos"
made of hay and bar-
rels, calf roping, and

MICHAELLA GALLINA

stick-horse racing. Thirty-five kids from all over the state joined in the rodeo. But nobody had more fun than Michaella: "It really makes you feel good knowing you are helping somebody else, knowing you're doing something that really makes a difference."[72]

To improve the quality of the day: That is the highest of the arts.

—Henry David Thoreau

⑥ Hero for All Time

Y ou know," I say, watching the fire coals crackle in the hearth of our hut, "this place is almost perfect."

Your eyes lift from the mug of cinnamon spice tea in your hands. "Almost?"

"Almost."

You take a sip. "What's missing? We have a roof over our heads, a decent meal in our bellies, and a chimney that doesn't blow over in every storm."

Grabbing the poker, I stir the embers. Sparks rise, and the air smells more smoky. Herc, curled up by the hearth, slaps his bushy tail on the floor.

"Bet he thinks we're going to roast marshmallows." I grin. "He must be the only dog alive who eats them."

"Come on," you plead. "What's missing?"

I draw a deep breath. "A picture on the wall. Not of a place, but a person. Someone we admire."

"Someone like Herc?"

The tail slaps again.

"No, no. I'm serious! To give this place the right feeling, it needs that extra . . . well, inspiration. We need a picture of someone special. Someone who will give us hope and courage whenever things get tough."

"You mean a hero."

"That's right, but not just any hero. We want someone who has really stood the test of time."

Slowly, you nod. "A hero for all time."

As a kid in rural Colorado, I didn't expect the school bus to come anywhere near our ranch house. In fact, it seemed almost miraculous that the bus stopped only about a mile away, at the end of our old ranch road.

This didn't make it any easier, mind you, for me to catch it every morning. No, just the opposite. Especially with my bag of books that felt about as light as a slab of petrified wood. Sometimes I had to run that road so fast I really wished I were Glenn Cunningham.

But after school, on the way home, things were different. No more rush. My homework could wait. I just plodded slowly up the road, watching a grazing antelope or a soaring red-tailed hawk. And my favorite thing to watch: the great blue expanse of the sky. That sky was so big, so wide, it seemed almost endless. And somehow . . . it made me feel bigger, too. Full of possibilities. With no limits on what I could do, where I could go, or what I could become.

And at night, the western sky seemed even more vast. I'd

step outside some evenings, when man-made sounds had retreated, and all I could hear were a few spring peepers or the distant neigh of a horse. I could see no lights but the dim glow of Colorado Springs on the horizon, and above my head, more stars than I could possibly hope to count. Huge, unfathomed sweeps of stars, shining bright.

Looking up at them, I felt incredibly small—and, at the same time, incredibly large. Small, because I was merely one creature, alive for just an instant compared to the eons-long life of a star. And large, because I was still connected to all those bright lights. Part of the same universe, the same Creation.

The same sky.

Now, the many heroes we've met in this book are themselves bright lights. They can guide us, just as the constellations guided travelers of old. They can light our way. And they can also inspire us to reach beyond ourselves, to dream of our own possibilities—possibilities as vast as the wide western sky.

What's more, like the stars overhead, the heroes in this book are wondrously diverse: all sizes, colors, and intensities. I have only mentioned a small sampling of the young men and women who have been heroes on the spot, survivor heroes, heroes within, and heroes to others near and far. Yet you can readily see that they belong to every gender, every culture, every origin. And on top of the diversity of their faces and their backgrounds is the great diversity of their accomplishments, the many ways they have enriched the world.

There are so many ways to be a hero! That's why there are countless examples of real heroism, both in contemporary life and in history. And in fiction, too. Just think, for example, of how many different kinds of heroic leaders live in our stories—

from King Arthur, the boy who dared to dream of Camelot; to Urnalda, the powerful queen of the dwarves; to Quetzalcoatl, the wise dragon who taught Aztecs how to grow maize; and to Huang Ti, the legendary Chinese emperor who could travel to other worlds through his dreams. And those are just a few.

With all this variety, it's perfectly fair to ask whether heroes really have *anything* in common. In other words, does the basic question I posed at the beginning of this book—What does it really take to be a hero?—truly have an answer?

Yes, it does. For despite their many differences, heroes share some enduring qualities of character. Those qualities, in fact, *define* their heroism.

We have seen those qualities many times in these pages. Now, some of them are stronger in certain kinds of heroes than others. Heroes within, for example, show an unbending faith in themselves that helps them climb their inner mountains. But for heroes on the spot, that quality isn't so important. For them, what matters more is a deep-rooted, instinctive sense of compassion. On the other hand, both these kinds of heroes need plenty of courage. And perseverance, too—whether that means fighting for years to triumph over polio, or fighting for just one more minute to save someone's life.

Here are seven of those enduring qualities—qualities that go to the very heart of heroism:

Courage. We've seen this quality in many forms, whether it's Melinda Clark plunging back into her burning house to save her little brother, or Ruby Bridges marching up the steps of her school despite an angry mob. Every hero makes a choice—a difficult choice, full of danger and possibly sacrifice.

Think of Pocahontas, who risked everything to save a fellow human being. Or Iqbal Masih, who did so much to alert the world to the horrors of child slavery. Or Theresa Prekerowa, who defied the Nazis . . . just to help a girl she didn't know. Each of them could have chosen an easier trail. But instead, they all chose another, more difficult trail—one that led to higher ground.

Faith. What a crucial quality this is! Whether it's faith in oneself, or in life's tendency to work toward the best, or in a higher power—or all three combined—it can make a great difference. Remember Wilma Rudolph, who simply *knew* down inside that she would walk again . . . and run like the wind? Or Joshua Dennis, who raised his voice in song even after days alone in that underground shaft? That's the power of such faith. And it's especially strong if it's found in someone of positive spirit—who refuses to be a victim, who takes responsibility for his or her life, and who sees past the struggles of today to the opportunities of tomorrow. Someone like Helen Keller, whose walls of darkness became wide open windows.

Perseverance. Most of the heroes we've met weren't just brave. They *stayed* brave for as long as it took to make a difference. Often enough, to save someone's life. That's why Sherwin Long's younger brother, who nearly drowned in the pool, is alive today. And why Andrew Holleman's cherished forest, that would have been destroyed, is still standing. This quality—call it, if you like, stick-to-it-ivity—can be the engine that carries a hero all the way to success. For the trail to success is often long and treacherous, much like the one that Sundiata walked when he led his west African people to freedom.

Hope. Beyond everything else, this quality is what empowered Anne Frank. It's what kept her writing about a new life, a brighter future, when most of what she saw around her was suffering and death. Like an underground spring that can't be suppressed, hope itself is a force. And also a kind of sustenance, an elixir of strength. Hope is what coaxed Stephen Hawking to explore the wide universe from his hospital bed. It's what made Prateep Ungsongtham Hata create her school in the slums of Bangkok. And it's what enabled Fox Beyer to play baseball, despite his disability: For him, cerebral palsy is just a curveball thrown at him by life, and he's going to keep right on swinging until he hits one out of the park.

Humor. If you can laugh at your problems, you can often master them. And if you can laugh at yourself—well, then you're likely to survive most anything. That's because humor requires a degree of distance, of separation, from whatever challenge you may face. With that separation comes perspective, objectivity, and maybe even a bit of wisdom. So when Abraham Lincoln poked fun at his hardships, he was really fending them off, giving himself the distance he needed. And when Satchel Paige joked about never looking back, he wasn't just talking about sports. He was talking, as a major league survivor, about life.

Adaptability. Trees that outlast the fiercest mountain storms are surprisingly flexible. Their trunks and limbs are strong, of course—but they are also able to bend with the harshest winds. By contrast, trees that are too stiff to bend often snap under pressure. It's like that for heroes. Just think of how Ohiyesa of the Sioux tribe survived when life's winds changed so drastically and made him Charles Eastman. Or how Ben MacDonald did whatever he needed to do (including eating uncooked frogs) to live like a badger. Despite everything they endured, these lads kept themselves alive—not just in body, but what is sometimes harder, in spirit.

Moral Direction. Just like Prometheus, who gave fire to the ancient Greeks, many young heroes have faced a profoundly difficult choice between their own personal safety and some greater good. To find their way through this labyrinth, they have relied on a compass inside themselves—a moral compass—and followed its bearings. Sometimes, the effect has been dramatic, as Ruby Bridges, Iqbal Masih, and Prateep Ungsongtham Hata have shown. A moral compass also guided those second-graders in California who worked so hard to save elephants from extinction. It spurred Valerie Edwards and Erin Scheide to change Maryland's laws on drunk driving. And it directed Ryan Hreljac to do everything in his power to bring clean drinking water to a village in Uganda. By following their inner compass, these heroes have changed the course of their lives . . . and the world, as well.

Taken together, these seven qualities constitute the key ingredients of heroism. If you could boil all of them down to their essence, mix them together in a great stew pot, and cook them over time, what a wondrous feast you'd have! Just one spoonful would be enough to empower a lifetime of heroic deeds.

Sometimes, heroes that powerful really do come along. They don't just show the qualities we've discussed—they come to symbolize, almost define, those qualities. In a very real way, they *become* those qualities.

Heroes of this kind are especially important to humanity.

The combination of who they are down inside, the time and place in which they live, and the particular feats they accomplish, identifies them with a certain heroic quality or mix of qualities. They lodge themselves deeply in our hearts and minds. And give us ongoing reminders of just how far we can walk, how high we can climb.

Individuals who transcend to this level are really a distinct kind of hero. They are *heroes for all time*. In the constellations of people who have made a difference in our lives, they are the brightest stars of all.

Why? What is it about them that sets them apart? In a word, *inspiration*. Their lives, their choices, their struggles—and, most of all, the heroic qualities they embody—have struck a soul-deep chord in humanity. A chord that reverberates across all barriers of time, culture, and language. These people have names like Abraham Lincoln, Anne Frank, Wilma Rudolph, Winston Churchill, Jane Goodall, the Dalai Lama, Mother Teresa, Nelson Mandela, Helen Keller, or Mohandas Gandhi.

But their true name is simply Hero. They remind us of our highest potential, our best selves. Yes, and of our own possibilities for heroism—possibilities as vast as the wide western sky.

We can perhaps do no great things; but we can do many small things with great love.

—Mother Teresa

⑦ Conclusion: The Hero Comes Home

I follow you and Herc out the door of our hut. Already, the first rosy rays of dawn are touching the treetops. When I shut the door behind us, the latch snaps tight. Our little hut seems just as solid as the mountain on which it stands.

"Whew," you say with a sigh, blowing a cloud in the frosty air. "What a great hike this was."

"A great journey."

You nod, then smile just a little. "And now it's time to go home."

Every hike must come to an end. You may be tired, sore, and hungry enough to eat your backpack. But you're also glad for the experience—and stronger because of it. Maybe even a little bit wiser.

The same is true for the hero's journey. When a hero comes home, battered but triumphant, it's time to get back to the everyday world. But the world is somehow different, somehow better, for his or her choices. Because that's what heroes do: They change the world. It may be in small, unnoticed ways, or in grand ways for all time. In every case, though, they make a positive difference.

Now, as we've seen, a hero's impact may be small indeed. So small that no one else notices. Yet it still matters. Maybe even a lot.

I'm reminded of a story about a girl who lived by the seashore. She loved to wander along the beach, exploring tide pools and watching the surf. One day she found that the tide had washed ashore hundreds and hundreds of starfish. They would die, she knew, unless returned soon to the water. So she decided to carry them, one by one, into the shallows of the sea, even if it took her all day long.

Just as she picked up her first starfish, a friend arrived. He asked what she was doing—and when she explained, he burst out laughing. "There are so many of them!" he exclaimed. "You can't possibly make any difference."

She plodded over to the water's edge and dropped in the starfish. Then she turned back to her friend. "I made a difference to that one."

Sometimes great heroism happens in everyday life. In the tiny, courageous choices it takes just to get through the day. To help someone in need. To lift someone's spirits. To give someone a hand—or a hug.

These are things anyone can do. For every single one of us has the capacity to make important choices, to do something remarkable . . . whether it's in our wider community, our own home, or our own self.

We have met many extraordinary people in the pages of this book. More than anything else, hearing about such diverse, heroic people reminds us that our choices really do matter. And because of that, we ourselves matter. Every single one of us, every single day.

Years ago, before I started writing books, I spent several years managing a business. It was a good, challenging job, and it taught me a few things about how to finance, produce, and sell products to people—the folks economists like to call *consumers*. You've heard the term, I'm sure: consumer products, consumer spending, and the like.

Trouble was, the term never seemed right to me. For if you call everyone a consumer, you're implying that all they do (or at least all they do for the economy) is consume things, devour products, and use up resources. Now, that's partly true, of course—even for people who are the most frugal and least wasteful. But it's certainly not the whole truth. People don't just consume things. They also create things, build things, and give things to others. They invent, protect, save, celebrate, share, nurture, and honor things, too.

In fact, we are more than just consumers. Much, much more. Let's think of ourselves, instead, as *creators*. Of our own lives. Our own communities. And yes, our own world.

That is really the essence of heroism: To take ourselves— our lives—seriously enough to make a mark. To leave a footprint on the trail. And by doing that, to change the trail for all who may come after.

Have a great hike! May you walk boldly and thoughtfully. And may you walk, as well, on the hero's trail.

More Quotations for the Trail

Never, never, never give up. —Winston Churchill

How wonderful it is that nobody need wait a single moment before starting to improve the world. —Anne Frank

All the rivers run into the sea; yet the sea is not full; but the place from whence the rivers come, thither they return again. —Ecclesiastes 1:7

Fall seven times, stand up eight. —Japanese proverb

Always do right. This will gratify some people, and astonish the rest. —Mark Twain

Whatever affects one directly, affects all indirectly. —Martin Luther King, Jr.

I have been terrified every day of my life, but that has never stopped me from doing everything I wanted to do. —Georgia O'Keefe

Whatever you are, be a good one. —Abraham Lincoln

Tell me what you pay attention to, and I will tell you who you are. —José Ortega y Gassett

We who lived in concentration camps can remember the men who walked through the huts comforting others, giving away their last piece of bread. . . . They offer sufficient proof that everything can be taken from a man but one thing: the last of the human freedoms—to choose one's attitude, to choose one's own way.   —Viktor Frankl

Our life is what our thoughts make it.   —Marcus Aurelius

Do what you can where you are with what you have.
                                        —Theodore Roosevelt

I'll walk where my own nature would be leading. It vexes me to choose another guide.   —Emily Brontë

Only within burns the fire I kindle.
My heart the altar, my heart the altar.
                                        —Poem of a Buddhist nun

We shall not cease from explorations; and the end of all our exploring will be to arrive where we started . . . and know the place for the first time.   —T. S. Eliot

What is a hero without a love for mankind?
                                        —Doris Lessing

The real voyage of discovery consists not in seeing new land-scapes, but in having new eyes.   —Marcel Proust

Too much of a good thing can be wonderful. —Mae West

Whatever you can do, or dream you can do, begin it. Boldness has genius and power in it. —Goethe

Character—the willingness to accept responsibility for one's own life—is the source from which self-respect springs. —Joan Didion

It would be a mistake to ascribe creative power to an inborn talent. Creativity takes courage. —Henri Matisse

Accuse not Nature, she hath done her part; do thou but thine! —John Milton

The best thing about the future is that it comes only one day at a time. —Abraham Lincoln

I have reached a point in my life where I understand the pain and the challenges, and my attitude is to stand with open arms to meet them all. —Myrlie Evers

Doing the best at this moment puts you in the best place for the next moment. —Oprah Winfrey

The world is indeed full of peril, and in it there are many dark places. But still there is much that is fair, and though in all lands love is now mingled with grief, it grows perhaps the greater. —J. R. R. Tolkien

We were born to make manifest the glory of God that is within us. —Nelson Mandela

It does not interest me what you do for a living: I want to know what you ache for, and if you dare to dream . . . for the adventure of being alive. —Oriah Mountain Dreamer

Look to this day, for it is life. —Sufi proverb

I shall always be grateful that my childhood was passed in a spot where there were many trees . . . old ancestral trees, planted and tended by hands long dead, bound up with all the joy and sorrow that visited the lives in their shadow. —L. M. Montgomery

The man who fears no truth has nothing to fear from a lie. —Thomas Jefferson

The ultimate lesson all of us have to learn is unconditional love, which includes not only others but ourselves as well. —Elizabeth Kübler-Ross

The most beautiful thing we can experience is the mysterious. It is the source of all true art and science. —Albert Einstein

Most things worth doing in the world had been declared impossible before they were done. —Louis Brandeis

No one can make you feel inferior without your consent.
—Eleanor Roosevelt

It is not only what we do, but what we do not do, for which we are accountable.
—Molière

Even if I knew the world would end tomorrow, I would plant an apple tree today.
—Martin Luther

Life is what we make it—always has been, always will be.
—Grandma Moses

All we can do during our lives is to leave a trace. We can leave it on a piece of paper, or on the ground, or in the hearts and minds of others.
—Elie Wiesel

I don't want to get to the end of my life and find that I just lived the length of it. I want to have lived the width of it as well.
—Diane Ackerman

It is better to light one candle than to curse the darkness.
—Chinese proverb

There is nothing in a caterpillar that tells you it's going to be a butterfly.
—Buckminster Fuller

Life loves to be taken by the lapel and told: "I am with you, kid. Let's go."
—Maya Angelou

What is now proved was once only imagined.
—William Blake

I am not afraid of storms, for I am learning to sail my ship.
—Louisa May Alcott

Count each day as a separate life.   —Seneca

Never doubt that a small group of concerned citizens can change the world. Indeed, it is the only thing that ever has.
—Margaret Mead

We make a living by what we get, but we make a life by what we give.   —Winston Churchill

Go confidently in the direction of your dreams.
—Henry David Thoreau

To be a leader you must feel that you are both everything and nothing—nothing in that you are on this Earth for a few years out of billions . . . everything, because you are at the center of all activity in your world.   —Edith Weiner

The invariable mark of wisdom is to see the miraculous in the common.   —Ralph Waldo Emerson

Compassion is the universal religion.   —The Dalai Lama

All things are connected. Whatever befalls the Earth befalls the children of the Earth.　　　　　　—Chief Seattle

Everywhere life is full of heroism.　　　　　—Desiderata

Acknowledgments

The author gratefully acknowledges these and other sources of information:

The Barefoot Book of Heroic Children, used by permission of Barefoot Books Ltd., © 2000 by Rebecca Hazell.

"Boy of Action," by Steve Dougherty and Vickie Bane in *People Weekly*, Time, Inc., © 1995.

Excerpt of "Burned Girl Gets a Hand from Veteran Fund-raiser" used by permission from the September 14, 2000, edition of *The Aurora Sentinel*.

Campbell, Joseph, *The Hero with a Thousand Faces*. Copyright © 1949 by Bollingen. Renewed 1976 by Princeton University Press. Reprinted by permission of Princeton University Press.

"Doing For Others," by Karen Vigel, in the March 19, 2001, issue of *The Pueblo Chieftain*.

Eastman, Charles, *Indian Heroes and Great Chieftains*. Used by permission of Dover Publications, Inc., © 1997.

Kids with Courage: True Stories about Young People Making a Difference, by Barbara A. Lewis, © 1992. Used with permission from Free Spirit Publishing, Inc., Minneapolis; 1-800-735-7323; *www.freespirit.com*. All rights reserved.

Through My Eyes, © 1999 by Ruby Bridges. Used with permission from Scholastic, Inc., with additional quote from the *New York Times* on 11/15/1960, © 2001 by the *New York Times*. Reprinted by permission.

Yoshiyama Award for Exemplary Service to the Community presented each year by the Hitachi Foundation to high-school seniors nationwide.

Young Heroes in World History, © 1999 by Robin Kadison Berson. Reproduced with permission of Greenwood Publishing Group, Inc., Westport, Conn.

Notes

1. Joseph Campbell, *The Hero with a Thousand Faces* (Princeton, New Jersey: Princeton University Press, 1949), 3.
2. The Max Warburg Courage Awards [Web site] 1998; http://www. maxcourage.org/essays/2000LongS.cfm.
3. Barbara A. Lewis, *Kids with Courage* (Minneapolis: Free Spirit Publishing, 1992), 110.
4. Nancy Vittorini, *Everyday Heroes* (New York: The Continuum Publishing Company, 2000), 18.
5. Ibid., 30.
6. Jim Namiotka, "A Shot of Adrenalin," *Reader's Digest* (May 1996): 65.
7. Lewis, 97.
8. Ibid., 103.
9. *The Oxford Reference Bible, King James Version, Esther 8:16* (Oxford, England: Oxford University Press, 1999).
10. Armstrong Sperry, *Call It Courage* (New York: Aladdin Books, an imprint of MacMillan Publishing Company, 1940), 94.
11. Robin Kadison Berson, *Young Heroes in World History* (Westport, Connecticut: Greenwood Press, 1999), 77–86.
12. Lewis, 126.
13. Leroy (Satchel) Paige, as told to David Lipman, *Maybe I'll Pitch Forever* (Lincoln, Nebraska: University of Nebraska Press, 1993), 14, 16, 21.
14. Ibid., 294.
15. Joslyn Pine, ed., *Wit and Wisdom of the American Presidents: A Book of Quotations* (Mineola, New York: Dover Publications, 2001), 27.
16. Ruby Bridges, *Through My Eyes* (New York: Scholastic Press, 1999), 4.
17. *New York Times*, 15 November, 1960. In Bridges, 16.
18. Phillip Hoose, *It's Our World, Too!* (Boston, New York, Toronto, London: Little Brown, 1993), 17–25.
19. Berson, 123–28.
20. Anne Frank, *Anne Frank: The Diary of a Young Girl* (New York: Simon & Schuster, 1952), 237.
21. Lewis, 47.

22. The Hitachi Foundation—Yoshiyama Award for Exemplary Service to the Community [Web page] 2001; http://www.hitachi.yoshiyama_1999/Sokhoeun_Chhunn.htm.

23. Lori Teresa Yearwood, "Archie Against the Odds," *Reader's Digest* (October 1999): 102.

24. Vittorini, 56.

25. Berson, 119.

26. Lewis, 27–29.

27. The Official Site for the Louis Armstrong House and Archives [Web site] 2001; http://independentmusician.com/louis/biography.php3.

28. Rebecca Hazell, *The Barefoot Book of Heroic Children* (New York: Barefoot Books, 2000), 68–73.

29. Barlow Meyers, *Champions All the Way* (Racine, Wisconsin: Whitman Publishing Company, 1944), 31–51.

30. Tim Folger, "The Ultimate Vanishing," *Discover* (October 1993): 100.

31. The Max Warburg Courage Awards [Web site] 1998; http://www.maxcourage.org/essays/2000DeratJ.cfm.

32. Ibid.

33. Vittorini, 58.

34. Peter Michelmore, "Born to Win," *Reader's Digest* (April 1999): 62–68.

35. Meyers, 209.

36. Hazell, 12–19.

37. Helen Keller, *Helen Keller: The Story of My Life* (New York: Penguin, Signet Classic, 1988, with an introduction by Lou Ann Walker, 1988), 18.

38. The Terry Fox Foundation [Web site] 2002. http://www.terryfoxrun.org [accessed 3 January, 2002].

39. David R. Boyd, *The Globe and Mail* (29 December, 2001): A14.

40. Vittorini, 43.

41. Meyers, 138–47.

42. Hazell, 82–87.

43. Lance Armstrong On-line [Web site] 2001; http://www.lancearmstrong.com [accessed 10 December, 2001].

44. Matthew Joseph Thaddeus Stepanek, *Heartsongs* (Alexandria, Virginia: VSP Books, 2001), 27.

45. Lewis, 73–79.

46. Geerat Vermeij, *Privileged Hands* (New York: W. H. Freeman and Company, 1997), 27.

47. Geocities [Web site] 2001; www.geocities.com/Vienna/1066/perlman.html.

48. Jone Johnson Lewis, Wisdom Quotes [Web site] 1996–2000; http://www.wisdomquotes.com [accessed 29 May, 2001].

49. Toby Axelrod, *Rescuers Defying the Nazis: Non-Jewish Teens Who Rescued Jews* (New York: The Rosen Publishing Group, Inc., 1999), 23.

50. Ibid.

51. Marlene Targ Brill, *Allen Jay and the Underground Railroad (On My Own)* (Minneapolis, Minnesota: Lerner Publishing Group, First Avenue Editions, 1993).

52. Vincent Harding, *Hope and History* (Maryknoll, New York: Orbis Books, 1990).

53. Ellen Levine, *Freedom's Children* (New York: Puffin Books, a division of Penguin Putnam, 1993), 31.

54. Vittorini, 82.

55. Barry Staver, "Boy of Action," *People* (June 19, 1995): 121–22.

56. Barron Prize [Web site] 2001; http://www.barronprize.org [accessed 29 May, 2001].

57. "Lending a Hand," *People* (10 October, 2001): 50–51.

58. Page Ivey, "South Carolina Children Repay Debt of Kindness," *Daily Herald* (11 November, 2001): A15.

59. Vittorini, 37.

60. Lewis, 143–50.

61. Ibid. 135–42.

62. Berson, 209–22.

63. Ryan and Susan Hreljac, *Ryan's Well Foundation Newsletter:* Volume 1, Issue 1, Fall 2001.

64. Kathy Cook, "Ryan's Well," *Reader's Digest* (June 2001): 144A–144C.

65. Vittorini, 95.

66. Hoose, 49–55.

67. Jane Goodall, *The Chimpanzees I Love: Saving Their World and Ours* (New York: Scholastic Press, 2001), 71.

68. Vittorini, 75.

69. Hazell, 74–81.

70. iafrica [Web site] 2000; http://iafrica.com/news/features/187723.htm.

71. Saran Starbridge, "For Future Generations," *Living Planet* (Winter 2000): 50.
72. Karen Vigel, "Doing for Others," *Pueblo Chieftain* (19 March, 2001): 8A.

Bibliography

Aesop. *The Complete Fables.* New York: Penguin Putnam, Penguin Classics, 1998.

Alexander, Caroline. *The Endurance: Shackleton's Legendary Antarctic Expedition.* New York: Random House, 1998.

Alvarado, Ph.D., Rudolph Valier. *Critical Lives: The Life and Work of Thomas Edison.* Indianapolis: Alpha Books, 2002.

Armstrong, Lance. *It's Not About the Bike.* New York: Penguin Putnam, 2001.

Axelrod, Toby. *Rescuers Defying the Nazis: Non-Jewish Teens Who Rescued Jews.* New York: The Rosen Publishing Group, Inc., 1999.

Barron Prize [Web site] 2001: http://www.barronprize.org [accessed 29 May, 2001].

Barron, T. A. *Heartlight.* New York: Philomel Books, 1990.

———. *The Lost Years of Merlin.* New York: Philomel Books, 1996.

Berson, Robin Kadison. *Young Heroes in World History.* Westport, Connecticut: Greenwood Press, 1999.

Black Elk, Nicholas, as told through John G. Neihardt (Flaming Rainbow). *Black Elk Speaks.* Lincoln, Nebraska: University of Nebraska Press, 2000.

Block, Gay, and Malka Drucker. *Rescuers: Portraits of Moral Courage in the Holocaust.* New York: TV Books, 1992.

Boorstin, Daniel J. *The Creators: A History of Heroes and the Imagination.* New York: Random House, 1992.

Boyd, David R. *The Globe and Mail* (29 December, 2001): A14.

Bridges, Ruby. *Through My Eyes.* New York: Scholastic Press, 1999.

Brill, Marlene Targ. *Allen Jay and the Underground Railroad (On My Own).* Minneapolis: Lerner Publishing Group, First Avenue Editions, 1993.

Campbell, Joseph. *The Hero with a Thousand Faces.* Princeton, New Jersey: Princeton University Press, 1949.

Chadha, Yogesh. *Gandhi: A Life.* New York: John Wiley & Sons, 1999.

Chang, Jung. *Wild Swans: Three Daughters of China.* New York: Anchor Books, a division of Random House, Inc., 1991.

Chase, Mary Ellen. *The Bible and the Common Reader.* New York: MacMillan, 1944.

Clark, Kenneth. *Leonardo da Vinci*. Baltimore: Penguin, 1959.

Coles, M.D., Robert. *The Call of Service*. New York: Houghton Mifflin, 1993.

————. *Lives of Moral Leadership: Men and Women Who Have Made a Difference*. New York: Random House, 2000, 2001.

Cook, Kathy. "Ryan's Well." *Reader's Digest*, June 2001, 144A–144C.

Day, John. *Toward Freedom: The Autobiography of Hawaharlal Nehru*. New York: John Day, 1941.

De Sahagún, Bernardino. *Historia General de las Cosas de Nueva España*. Mexico, 1829, Lib. III, Cap.xii-xiv (condensed). The work has been republished by Pedro Robredo (Mexico, 1938), Vol. I, 278–82. In *The Hero with a Thousand Faces*. Joseph Campbell (Princeton, New Jersey: Princeton University Press, 1949), p. 359.

Detrich, Terry and John. *The Spirit of Lo: An Ordinary Family's Extraordinary Journey*. Tulsa, Oklahoma: Mind Matters, Inc., 2000.

Dorsey, George A., and Alfred L. Kroeber. *Traditions of the Arapaho* (Field Columbia Museum, Publication 81, Anthropological Series, Vol.V: Chicago, 1903), 300. Reprinted in Stith Thompson's *Tales of the North American Indians* (Cambridge, Massachusetts, 1929), 128. In *The Hero with a Thousand Faces*. Joseph Campbell (Princeton, New Jersey: Princeton University Press, 1949).

Douglass, Frederick. *Narrative of the Life of Frederick Douglass*. New York: Dover, 1995.

Eckert, Allan W. *Incident at Hawk's Hill*. New York: Bantam, 1971.

Einstein, Albert. *Ideas and Opinions*. New York: Crown, 1954.

Ellis, Joseph J. *American Sphinx: The Character of Thomas Jefferson*. New York: Vintage/Random House, 1996.

Folger, Tim. "The Ultimate Vanishing." *Discover*, October 1993, 98–106.

Frank, Anne. *Anne Frank: The Diary of a Young Girl*. New York: Simon & Schuster, 1952.

Franklin, Benjamin. *The Autobiography of Benjamin Franklin*. Mineola, New York: Dover, 1996.

Giles, Herbert A. *The Chinese Biographical Dictionary*. London and Shanghai: 1898, 372. In *The Hero with a Thousand Faces*. Joseph Campbell (Princeton, New Jersey: Princeton University Press, 1949), 189.

The Giraffe Project [Web site] 1995–2000: http://www.giraffe.org/heroes.html [accessed 29 May, 2001].

Glenn, John, with Nick Taylor. *John Glenn: A Memoir*. New York: Bantam, 1999.

Goodall, Jane. *The Chimpanzees I Love: Saving Their World and Ours*. New York, Scholastic, 2001.

Graham, Katherine. *Personal History*. New York: Knopf, 1997.

Haley, Gail E., retold. *A Story A Story: An African Tale*. New York: Atheneum, 1970.

Harding, Vincent. *Hope and History*. Maryknoll, New York: Orbis Books, 1990.

Hazell, Rebecca. *The Barefoot Book of Heroic Children*. New York: Barefoot Books, 2000.

Hertog, Susan. *Anne Morrow Lindbergh: Her Life*. New York: Anchor/ Random House, 1999.

His Holiness the Dalai Lama. *Ethics for the New Millennium*. New York: Riverhead/Penguin Putnam, 1999.

————. *Freedom In Exile: The Autobiography of the Dalai Lama*. San Francisco: Harper, 1991.

The Hitachi Foundation—Yoshiyama Award for Exemplary Service to the Community [Web site] 2001: http://www.hitachi.yoshiyama_1999/ 1999awardees.html [accessed 29 May, 2001].

Hoose, Phillip. *It's Our World, Too!* Boston, New York, Toronto, London: Little Brown, 1993.

Hreljac, Ryan and Susan. *Ryan's Well Foundation Newsletter:* Volume 1, Issue 1. Ontario, Canada: 2001.

iafrica [Web site] 2000; http://iafrica.com/news/features/187723.htm [accessed 10 October, 2001].

Ivey, Page. "South Carolina Children Repay Debt of Kindness." *Daily Herald*, 11 November, 2001, A15.

Jefferson County School District N. R-1. *Kids Explore: Kids Who Make a Difference*. Santa Fe, New Mexico: John Muir Publications, 1997.

Keller, Helen. *Helen Keller: The Story of My Life*. Introduction by Lou Ann Walker. New York: Penguin, Signet Classic, 1988.

Kennedy, John F. *Profiles in Courage—Memorial Edition*. New York: Harper & Row, 1964.

Lance Armstrong On-line [Web site] 2001: http://www.lancearmstrong. com [accessed 10 December, 2001].

Lansky, Bruce, ed. *Girls to the Rescue*. New York: Simon & Schuster, 1995.

Layden, Joe. *Against the Odds*. New York: Scholastic, 1997.

"Lending A Hand." *People*, October 2001.

Levine, Ellen. *Freedom's Children: Young Civil Rights Activists Tell Their Own Stories*. New York: Penguin Putnam Books for Young Readers, 2000.

Lewis, Barbara A. *Kids with Courage*. Minneapolis: Free Spirit Publishing, 1992.

Lewis, Jone Johnson. Wisdom Quotes [Web site] 1996–2000: http://www.wisdomquotes.com [accessed 29 May, 2001].

Lowry, Lois. *Number the Stars*. South Holland, Illinois: Dell, 1989.

Lucas, George. *Star Wars*. 121 min. Lucasfilm Ltd., 1977.

Malory, Sir Thomas. *Le Morte d'Arthur*. New York: Modern Library, 1994.

Manchester, William. *The Last Lion, Winston Spencer Churchill: Visions of Glory 1874–1932*. Boston: Little, Brown, 1983.

Mandela, Nelson. *Long Walk to Freedom: The Autobiography of Nelson Mandela*. New York: Little, Brown, 1995.

Martin, Katherine. *Women of Courage: Inspiring Stories from the Women Who Lived Them*. Novato, California: 1999.

The Max Warburg Courage Awards [Web site] 1998: http://www.maxcourage.org/essays/winners2000.cfm [accessed 29 May, 2001].

Meyers, Barlow. *Champions All the Way*. Racine, Wisconsin: Whitman Publishing Company, 1944.

Michelmore, Peter. "Born To Win." *Reader's Digest*, April 1999, 62–68.

Moeller, Bill and Jan. *Chief Joseph and the Nez Percés: A Photographic History*. Missoula, Montana: Mountain Press Publishing Company, 1995.

Munds, Tom. "Burned Girl Gets a Hand from Veteran Fund-raiser." *The Aurora Sun Sentinel*, 14 September, 2000, 5.

My Hero [Web site] 2000: http://www.myhero.com/hero.asp?hero=s_hawking [accessed 29 May, 2001].

Ibid.: http://www.myhero.com/hero.asp?hero=wilmaRudolf [accessed 29 May, 2001].

Namiotka, Jim. "A Shot of Adrenaline." *Reader's Digest*, May 1996, 65.

New York Times, 15 November, 1960. In Ruby Bridges. *Through My Eyes* (New York: Scholastic 1999), 16.

The Oxford Reference Bible, King James Version, Esther 8:16. Oxford, England: Oxford University Press, 1999.

Page, Michael, and Robert Ingpen. *Encyclopedia of Things That Never Were*. Surrey, Great Britain: Landsdowne Press, 1985.

Paige, Leroy (Satchel), as told to David Lipman. *Maybe I'll Pitch Forever.* Lincoln, Nebraska: University of Nebraska Press, 1993.

Philip, Neil. Retold. *The Arabian Nights.* New York: Orchard Books, 1994.

Pine, Joslyn, ed. *Wit and Wisdom of the American Presidents: A Book of Quotations.* Mineola, New York: Dover, Inc., 2001.

Roosevelt, Eleanor. *This Is My Story.* New York: Harper & Brothers, 1937.

Ryan's Well Foundation [Web site] 2001: http://www.ryanswell.ca [accessed 29 May, 2001].

Sandburg, Carl. *Abraham Lincoln: The Prairie Years and the War Years.* New York: Harcourt, Brace, 1974.

Schwab, Gustav. *Gods and Heroes: Myths and Epics of Ancient Greece.* New York: Random House, 1946.

Sperry, Armstrong. *Call It Courage.* New York: Aladdin Books/ MacMillan, 1940.

Sports Illustrated for Women [Web site] 2000: http://sportsillustrated. cnn.com/siforwomen/top_100/8/ [accessed 29 May, 2001].

Starbridge, Saran. "For Future Generations." *Living Planet* (Winter 2000): 50.

Staver, Barry. "Boy of Action." *People,* 19 June, 1995, 121–22.

Stepanek, Matthew Joseph Thaddeus. *Heartsongs.* Alexandria, Virginia: VSP Books, 2001.

Stuart, Jesse. *The Thread That Runs So True: A Mountain School Teacher Tells His Story.* New York: Scribner, 1949.

The Terry Fox Foundation [Web site] 2002: http://www.terryfoxrun.org [accessed 3 January, 2002].

Tolkien, J. R. R. *The Lord of the Rings.* New York: Houghton Mifflin, 1967.

Vermeij, Geerat. *Privileged Hands.* New York: Henry Holt, 1997.

Vigel, Karen. "Doing for Others." *Pueblo Chieftain,* 19 March, 2001, 8A.

Vittorini, Nancy. *Everyday Heroes.* New York: Continuum, 2000.

White, T. H. *The Once and Future King.* New York: Putnam, 1939, 1940.

Yearwood, Lori Teresa. "Archie Against the Odds." *Reader's Digest,* October 1999, 102.

Index

The Hero's Trail

131

A Reader's Guide to THE HERO'S TRAIL
by T.A. Barron

T.A. Barron's book, *The Hero's Trail*, is subtitled *A Guide for a Heroic Life*. Like all good guidebooks, this one points out features we might otherwise overlook, maps a route we might want to follow, but leaves the ultimate choices about what directions to take up to us, the reader—or to stay with Barron's metaphor, the traveler. *The Hero's Trail* can be read from the middle out, from the beginning to the end, from the end to the beginning, a little here, a little there. And like the best of guidebooks, you can return to it time and time again when you can't quite remember your way.

In a similar manner, this reader's guide is designed to point out some features you might have missed, and suggest a route for discussion. Feel free to read it in any order. I hope that it will help you and your fellow travelers on your chosen paths.

—Dr. Kylene Beers

1. T.A. Barron writes, "For despite their many differences, heroes share some enduring qualities of character. Those qualities, in fact, define their heroism" (page 98). He defines those qualities as:

Courage	*Perseverance*	*Adaptability*
Faith	*Hope*	*Moral Direction*
	Humor	

You can reread what Barron says about each of those qualities on pages 98–102.

Q: *Do you agree with this list of seven?*

Q: *What other qualities might you add to that list? What about intelligence? Popularity? Compassion?*

Q: *Can a person have the qualities Barron identifies and not be a hero? In other words, is it possible to be heroic and not be a hero?*

2. Think of someone, from real life or fiction, you consider to be a hero. What did that person do to make her or him a hero in your eyes? What do you most admire about that person? Of Barron's five kinds of heroes, what type of hero would that person be:

Hero on the spot	*Hero within*	*Hero to others*
Survivor hero	*Hero for all times*	*near and far*

3. What other heroes can you think of? And what types of hero would they be?

4. Barron writes, "For a hero, what counts is character. For a celebrity, what counts is fame" (page 3).
Q: *Do you agree with this?*
Q: *Make a quick list of people you consider to be heroes. Make another list of people you'd call celebrities. Are there any names that would show up on both lists? If so, what qualities did those people have that allow them to be both a hero and a celebrity?*

5. Sometimes a book is a window, offering a glimpse into a world beyond our own. Other times a book is a mirror, offering us the opportunity to see ourselves, to reflect on the choices we make. Would you say this book is a window or a mirror or both?

6. What do you think about what Barron wrote on page 9: "Heroes are more than companions on our journey. They remind us who we are, and who we can become. In truth, when we follow the hero's trail, we are entering into ourselves—into our hopes, struggles, fears, and ideals. Celebrating heroes is a terrific way to remember our own heroic potential."
Q: *How does celebrating a hero help you to find your own heroic potential?*
Q: *Which hero in this book would you most want to be like? What qualities draw you to that person? How can you try to make those qualities a part of your own life?*

7. Barron writes, "Here is a marvelous thing about faith: It can coexist with doubt. It can even grow stronger in the face of doubt" (page 59).
Q: *What does this mean?*
Q: *How could you have faith in yourself or someone else or something you believe and at the same time have doubts?*
Q: *Why would it be important to maintain your faith in those moments of doubt? Which of Barron's five kinds of hero (see the list above) most needs to maintain faith?*

8. Revisit the quotations that open each chapter. Discuss the following:
Q: *Which quotation do you like the most? Why?*
Q: *Barron matched quotations to chapters. How does each quotation fit with the chapter?*
Q: *Look at the additional quotations found on pages 107–113. Could any of those quotations have been set at the beginning of any chapters? Which ones?*

9. Some say that heroes are not made, but are born. In other words, you can't set out in life to become a hero; instead, there's something in you from birth that makes you heroic.

Q: *Do you agree with this statement? Why or why not?*

Q: *If you could sit and talk with T. A. Barron, do you think he'd agree with that statement?*

Q: *What in* The Hero's Trail *gives you insight into how Barron might respond?*

10. After reviewing the quotations at the end of the book, choose the ones you like most and do some investigative work to find out something about the people who said those quotes. Read about those people in an encyclopedia or go online to a search engine such as www.google.com and enter each person's name. After you've read about a person, discuss what you found and then decide if that person is a hero.

11. Barron writes, "Sometimes great heroism happens in everyday life. In the tiny, courageous choices it takes just to get through the day. To help someone in need. To lift someone's spirits. To give someone a hand—or a hug" (page 104). What courageous choices do you make every day?

Q: *How can peer pressure work against making courageous choices?*

Q: *What happens when we choose the less courageous choices?*

12. Robert Frost wrote a poem titled "The Road Not Taken" that in part says: "Two roads diverged in a wood and I—I took the one less traveled by/ And that has made all the difference." What do these lines mean to you? What difference could it make in your life to travel the less-traveled road? How do these lines fit with what Barron is saying about making "courageous choices"?

The reader's guide for *The Hero's Trail* was written by Kylene Beers, Ed.D.
She is a Senior Reading Researcher for the
School Development Program at Yale University.